Science-Based Social Skills:
Using Psychological Data to Beat Awkwardness, Survive Small Talk, and Win People Over

By Patrick King

Social Interaction and Conversation Coach at
www.PatrickKingConsulting.com

Table of Contents

INTRODUCTION — 9

SOCIAL SKILLS MATTER MORE THAN YOU THINK — 12

CHAPTER 1: SETTING THE FOUNDATION — 17

YOUR TEEN YEARS SET THE SOCIAL STAGE — 17
IT'S NEVER TOO LATE TO LEARN — 20
STRAIGHTEN OUT YOUR EXPECTATIONS — 25
UNDERSTANDING THE "LIKING GAP" — 29
SELF-FULFILLING SOCIAL PERCEPTIONS — 35

CHAPTER 2: PLAYING THE SOCIAL GAME — 41

SOCIAL LEARNING AND POPULARITY — 41
WHAT MAKES A PERSON POPULAR? — 46
DON'T BE DOWN ON YOURSELF — 49
BE CAREFUL WITH SOCIAL COMPARISONS — 55
BE REAL… BUT MINDFUL OF YOUR PRESENTATION — 61

CHAPTER 3: GETTING IN SYNC — 67

FACIAL EXPRESSIVITY AND SOCIAL SUCCESS — 67
SEND GOOD VIBES BY SMILING — 71
MOODS ARE CONTAGIOUS — 75
THE CHEMISTRY FORMULA — 80

CHAPTER 4: WHAT FRIENDSHIPS ARE MADE OF — 87

DISPLAY COMMONALITY — 87
WHAT MAKES PEOPLE BOND? — 91

FREQUENT, LOW-STAKES EXPOSURE	95
DO THINGS TOGETHER...	100
...BUT SCREEN TIME DOESN'T COUNT	103
BOND THROUGH SHARED EXPERIENCES	106
RECIPROCITY MATTERS MORE THAN PERFECTION	111

CHAPTER 5: TOOLS OF THE TRADE — 117

WHY FIRST IMPRESSIONS MATTER	117
PUT IN A GOOD WORD FOR YOURSELF	119
SAY PEOPLE'S NAMES	124
POLITENESS IS (USUALLY) THE DEFAULT	128
THE GAIN-LOSS THEORY OF ATTRACTION	131

CHAPTER 6: IT'S HOW YOU FRAME THINGS — 137

THE ART OF "SELF-HANDICAPPING"	137
HUMOR IS YOUR SECRET WEAPON	140
DON'T BE AFRAID TO ASK FOR HELP	146
CHEAT CODE: THE DOOR-IN-THE-FACE TECHNIQUE	156

CHAPTER 7: COMMON MISCONCEPTIONS — 161

SOCIALIZE—EVEN IF YOU DON'T ALWAYS FEEL LIKE IT!	161
MISERY LOVES (SIMILAR) COMPANY	165
THE ADVICE PARADOX	170
BE A CONFORMIST... BUT NOT WHEN IT REALLY MATTERS	175
KEEP CONVERSATIONALLY BALANCED	179

CHAPTER 8: THE ROMANCE ELEMENT — 185

THE SECRET TO AN ATTRACTIVE ONLINE DATING PROFILE	185
"WHAT SOUNDS BEAUTIFUL IS GOOD"	189
BE PROUD, NOT ARROGANT	194
TWEAK THE RECIPE	198
COMMUNAL VS. EXCHANGE RELATIONSHIPS	204
FACE-TO-FACE IS BEST	208

CHAPTER 9: BECOMING SOCIALLY INTELLIGENT 213

THREE TYPES OF SOCIAL CAPITAL	213
KEEP IT MUTUAL	217
THE TEN SOCIAL DIMENSIONS	220
DON'T BE RESPONSIBLE, BE RESPONSIVE	225
THE SECRET TO APPLIED EMPATHY	230

CHAPTER 10: THE HABITS OF THE SOCIALLY SUCCESSFUL 235

PRACTICE SMALL ACTS OF RELIABILITY	235
BE INTELLECTUALLY HUMBLE	240
THE ACTOR-OBSERVER BIAS	245
HOW LONG DOES IT TAKE TO MAKE A FRIEND?	249
MOLLENHORST'S SEVEN-YEAR FRIENDSHIPS	252

CONCLUSION 257

Introduction

Why bother acquiring excellent social skills?

That's easy: **Because healthy relationships are the key to happiness.**

Picture this. You come away from a particularly satisfying social situation and you feel *amazing*.

There's a spring in your step.

You feel energized and resilient.

You've had fun, you felt seen, and for a moment you forgot all about whatever was bothering you before.

Have you ever felt this way?

When a social interaction goes well, you feel like you belong, you feel connected, and you simply revel in that warm glow of life feeling good.

Many intelligent people intuitively understand that if they want to access something of value, they need to make an effort.

Want to make money? You'll need to find a way to offer the world something of value.

Want to win a competition or finish a marathon? You'll need to put in those hours of disciplined practice.

Yet when it comes to relationships——i.e., the things most of us already know are supremely valuable for life satisfaction—most of just wing it.

We passively assume that good intentions are enough, and that if we're broadly good people, then good relationships will just spontaneously develop along the way, right?

Wrong!

Every human being has a fundamental need for relationship. But that doesn't mean they know HOW.

- **How** do you actually get people to like and respect you?
- **How** do you stay true to yourself while still putting your best foot forward?
- **How** do you make chemistry happen? What even *is* chemistry?!
- **How** do you make friends, practically speaking, one step at a time?
- **How** do you communicate so that people actually *get* you?
- **How** do you get people to stick around once they've become your friend?

It doesn't matter if you're reading this book because you're yearning for more genuine conversation and human bonding, or (let's be honest) just because you want to be more popular.

Whatever your goals, here's the good news: **Social skills can be acquired.** You just need to know how.

No matter who you are, where you're starting from, or what obstacles you've faced in the past, you *can* learn to create a social life that is satisfying, rich, rewarding... and lots of fun.

What follows is a condensed collection of **evidence-based** practices, methods, and approaches that have **scientifically proven** connections to improved social skills.

It's simple:

- Improve social skills = better relationships.
- Better relationships = a happier life.

We'll be taking a close look at the latest research studies in the social sciences, extracting their core findings, then finding creative and intelligent ways to apply those principles to our own lives.

A good social life is *not* about luck. It's something that can be engineered.

Relationships don't just randomly fall out of the sky. They're cultivated, deliberately.

There's no big mystery to that magical "click" you feel with someone. Connecting with other people is something *anyone* can do, no matter your temperament.

Social skills matter more than you think

The 80-year long *Harvard Study of Adult Development* shows clearly that **good relationships are better predictors of lifetime happiness than any other variable—** —even money, success, social class, IQ, or genes (Mineo, April 2017, *Harvard Gazette*).

A study conducted by The University of British Columbia in Canada (led by social psychologist Dunigan Folk, 2025 study still to be peer-reviewed) used AI to analyze data from the 2013 and 2021 editions of the American Time Use Survey (ATUS). They wanted to investigate the way that people spread their time across different activities.

One of their most interesting findings? When participants reported a *really good day*, it tended to follow a predictable formula:

Apparently, the Best Day Ever includes a whopping 9.5 hours of socialization:

- 6 hours spent with family
- 2 hours spent with friends
- 1.5 hours additional socializing

(For those interested, the rest of the day included 2 hours of exercise, less than 6 hours of work and no more than 1 hour of screen time—no surprises there).

Importantly, these social hours are not just candlelit dinners and quality time. They include social interaction of all shades: small talk with cashiers, working alongside colleagues, idle chit chat, and miscellaneous "hanging out."

Now, regardless of how realistic or desirable that ideal seems, what's important is that the researchers were not directly asking about socializing—they merely studied the makeup of a typical day and noted which days people tended to rate as "above average."

The big takeaway: **Human beings need far, far more social interaction than they think!**

A day filled with connection is a day that's warmer, softer, lighter, and more fulfilling.

Let's put these two studies together:

- A happy life depends on successful, healthy relationships.
- The optimal time spent socializing with others is around 9.5 hours a day.

The message is clear: If we want a good life, we need to know how to manage our relationships——i.e., how to spend the bulk of our waking lives.

Social skills = happy life skills.

So, what's stopping you from having that "above average day" as your average day?

Everyone craves emotional support, connection, belonging, and shared emotional experiences. Yet we are also in the midst of what many call a "loneliness epidemic."

Why?

A 2020 study published in *Personality and Individual Differences* asked this very question: if human relationships are so very important, why do people fail so often to maintain them?

They identified 40 separate reasons and six different factors that keep people from satisfying social connections.

In the chapters that follow, we'll be taking a much closer look at each of these concepts—as well as many, many more. For now, let's paraphrase their findings into a quick cheat sheet.

What kind of people do we have to be to have good social lives?

Let's start with what ISN'T important.

Succeeding socially is *not*:

- **A competition.** To make friends you do not need to be:
  - Impressive or charismatic

- Dominant or forceful
- Super attractive
- Entertaining
- Intelligent
- **A negotiation**. To make friends you do not need to be:
  - Manipulative
  - Fake or less like the real you
  - Self-serving
  - Inauthentic
  - Influential

So, if you've been feeling inadequate, intimidated, or insecure about your own ability to succeed socially, let yourself off the hook—— *you probably already have everything you need* to be a great friend, acquaintance, partner, and colleague right now.

That's because the following things ARE important:

- Trust
- Genuine emotional connection and companionship
- Common values, compatible worldviews, and a few shared interests

That's it!

Fostering authentic emotional resonance and mutual understanding is the most effective way to build lasting relationships of

all kinds—and that's exactly what this book is about.

In the chapters that follow we'll be looking at HOW to create those feelings of trust, warmth, similarity, liking, and real connection.

We'll:

- Unpack and let go of old beliefs that are no longer serving us
- Pick up a few rules for how to play the social game
- Understand why syncing, sharing, and alignment are so important
- Figure out what makes good friendships, what they are, and how to cultivate them
- Explore social tricks and hacks to make you seem more likeable and trustworthy
- How to think and behave like a socially successful person

Charisma and funny stories? Not required!

All that you'll need is a little curiosity, a sense of playfulness, and a willingness to proactively try some of the suggested action steps.

If you're ready, let's dive in.

Chapter 1: Setting the foundation

Your teen years set the social stage

Did you have a best friend when you were a teenager?

Cast your mind back to when you were 15 years old...

Who played a big role in your world back then?

And how does your life look today in comparison?

In a recent study published in *Social Cognitive and Affective Neuroscience* (Dauvermann et. al., 2024) researchers at the University of Birmingham showed that **teenage friendships are a significant influence on adult mental health**.

The quality of your friendships at around 14 –18 years of age, the authors claim, is actually a great predictor of future mental health and resilience against trauma.

Here's what the research team did:

- They gathered a group of more than a thousand young people who had all experienced childhood trauma.
- These participants completed a Cambridge Friendship Questionnaire at different time periods:
  - age 13-14
  - age 17-18
  - age 24
- The team also attempted to measure resilience by seeing how well people responded to social exclusion.
- Finally, some of the remaining participants also received brain imaging (and fMRI scan) at age 24.

Their findings were fascinating:

- Overall, a higher score on the Cambridge Friendship Questionnaire at age 13-14 was significantly associated with *better mental health* at age 24, as well as *greater psychological resilience.*
- The differences were even apparent in the fMRI scans, which revealed healthier brain responses in stressful social situations.

In short, healthy teenage friendships predict better outcomes in adulthood.

For the younger group (13-14) healthy friendships generally mean feeling accepted by the group.

For the older group (17-18) healthy friendships are more about quality than quantity. Even just one or two very close friends predict better success in work, romance, and life in general as an adult.

These findings concur with those of another study (Winding et. al., 2025, *"Adolescent friendships and their impact on self-rated health in early adulthood. A prospective cohort study"*).

Their main discovery? Having a close friend at age 15 almost doubled the odds of reporting good health at 29. These effects were most pronounced for teen friendships, which appeared to be more influential and foundational than later adult friendships.

There are a few insights we can glean from this research:

- **It's quality over quantity.** You can enjoy the health and wellness benefits of friendship even if you only have one or two very close friends.
  - While quantity matters more when we're young, quality matters more to us as we get older.
  - It's OK not to have a "best friend" as an adult—in fact, it's normal not to maintain the intensity of early adolescent friendships as an adult.
- **If you've struggled with making friends as an adult, cut yourself some slack.**

- Do you find socializing hard and a little mystifying? You simply may have missed out on some of those formative, resilience-creating friendships. Be kind to yourself. Instead of beating yourself up for not being more socially successful, give yourself the support you need now as an adult.
- Quick tip: Start by casting your social net wide, and then gradually focus on the one or two deeper, more intimate friendships—that's more than enough!

Action step: Reflect on the lessons you learned during your childhood and teenage years. How might these early formative experiences have influenced your beliefs about socializing as an adult?

It's never too late to learn

People are innately sociable... but that doesn't mean they are born with all their social skills intact.

Think of a baby. It's born with all the equipment needed to walk—two legs—but it takes time and practice to learn to use those legs! A baby will learn to walk best when it is supported and encouraged to do what it is naturally born to do.

It's the same with social skills. We're all born with the cognitive, emotional, and behavioral hardware necessary to connect with our fellow human beings, but this is potential that needs to be made actual.

Like the baby, we need support and encouragement to learn to do what we're naturally born to do.

Social competence is shaped by:

- Your early experiences
- The caregiving you receive
- The extent to which your biological needs are met

But it doesn't stop there!

We develop social competence all throughout life. It's a continuous development.

This is good news because it means that as long as we are alive, we can continue to learn, experience, develop, and grow. Pop psychology tends to zoom in on childhood traumas and shortcomings, but the truth is that you can always improve your social skills in adulthood, no matter what might have occurred in the past.

What does the research tell us?

Early childhood experiences lay the foundations for later social competence (Luecken, Roubinov & Tanaka, 2013).

- We all need to learn who we are, how to relate to others, and how to communicate

and feel empathy. How? Our primary caregivers model it for us.
- What we learn in childhood is carried with us all throughout the rest of our lives.
- Secure early attachment is associated with the best adult social outcomes (Bowlby, 1944)

So... what happens if you *didn't* have secure attachments or good role models growing up? Are you doomed to adult social incompetence?

Thankfully, no. **Your childhood matters, but it's not *all* that matters.**

One study, (Nellis et. al., 2011, *Emotion*), found that certain skills could actually be trained in adults—just 18 hours on a specially targeted training program (plus email follow-up) significantly improved participants' social skills.

Emotional competence training has been shown to increase extraversion and agreeableness while decreasing neuroticism (three of the "Big 5" personality traits), as well as improve overall wellbeing, increase employability, and even reduce cortisol levels—effects that persisted for a year or longer (Kotsou, 2011, *Journal of Applied Psychology*).

What did these training programs focus on?

1. Warmth
2. Boundaries

3. Self-regulation

Luecken et al. find that our early childhood experiences are so influential *because they impart us with the above three capacities*. That means that if you weren't taught these things then, there's still time to learn for yourself now. Feel like you've missed out on these early formative experiences? Don't worry—these three capacities are the place to start building.

Knowing how to emotionally self-regulate, to convey and receive warmth, and to maintain healthy boundaries are life skills that can be acquired. And that's exactly what this book is about.

A great place to start: Which of these core competencies do you find most challenging? Start there, and choose one small thing you can do today that will help you build a habit of competence over time.

- To cultivate more relational warmth:
    o Practice active listening – make eye contact, reflect back what you hear, ask questions, and make sure not to interrupt.
    o Use warm and open body language – i.e., smile! (We'll explore the magic of smiling later on).
    o Express genuine appreciation for others – give compliments and say thank you.

- Try asking people for help, support, and advice in small ways, and doing the same for them—this builds trust.
- To improve boundaries:
  - Take the time to clearly identify your own limits, whether the resource you are protecting is time, money, energy, or something else.
  - Practice writing down and speaking your boundaries out loud using "I" sentences that express your limits and needs without blame or shame ("I need to have a few hours on the weekends to just be alone").
  - In the same way, practice saying *no* without explanation, justification, or apology. Find small things that you can firmly, yet politely, assert your boundaries on, before working up to bigger boundaries.
- To build emotional regulation:
  - Get into the habit of pausing often—just a few seconds will do—to check in with yourself. Interrupt any impulsive or instinctive reactions you may be having, and gain awareness of where you are, what you're feeling, and what you're thinking.
  - Try to put a name on your emotion to gain some psychological distance ("I'm feeling lonely right now").

- Notice when you're out of balance and take steps to care for your physical, emotional, spiritual, and social wellbeing—exercise, reach out to a friend, meditate, sleep well, or pay a little more attention to your nutrition.

On the surface, these little everyday habits don't look like much, but they add up.

These capacities are not developed overnight, but gradually, over the course of a lifetime.

Whenever you consciously bring them to your relationships, you give yourself the chance learn to navigate a healthy, balanced way through social situations… even if your early foundations in this area have been a little patchy!

Action tip: Learning to be socially competent is a lifelong process, but it's the little things that count. Choose one small everyday social habit you'd like to cultivate (make it small!) and commit to taking one positive step in that direction today.

Straighten out your expectations

People who struggle socially can sometimes have severely limiting misconceptions about themselves and other people.

"I'm a loser who doesn't have enough friends."

"I have to work on myself before people will like me."

"Everyone else finds socializing easier than I do."

"I'm missing out."

TV, movies, and social media have distorted our expectations around social life and what it should look like. But let's see if we can take an objective view.

In her book *Friendship: The Evolution, Biology, and Extraordinary Power of Life's Fundamental Bond* author and science journalist Lydia Denworth explores the deeper evolutionary, biological, and psychosocial foundations for human friendship.

Denworth spoke with neuroscientists, geneticists, and medical professionals who each explain the profound effect that closeness has on human health and wellbeing.

Published the year the world went into Covid lockdown (2020), Denworth's book has plenty of interesting insights about connection, vulnerability, and loneliness in the age of social media.

Denworth analyzed scientific and social psychology studies by Dunbar, Lieberman, and others. She drew on longitudinal studies, fMRI data on social bonding, and evolutionary biology, especially Robin Dunbar's social brain hypothesis (which proposes a cognitive limit to stable social relationships of around 150 people).

Here's an extremely brief summary of what all this research boils down to:

- **Quality always matters more than quantity.** A single close, true friend has a more significant impact on mental and physical wellbeing than dozens of weak connections and superficial acquaintances.
- **It's vulnerability, not independence, that binds us together.** People don't connect in their perfection, but in their mutual need for and dependence on one another. Personal disclosures and honest revelations build trust and invite the other person to do the same (Aron et al., 1997).
- **Friendships increase resilience and survival.** Having a robust social network lowers your risk of illness, neurodegenerative disease, and premature death—*more than even exercising or quitting smoking does.*

What's interesting is to notice the way that Denworth's recommendations contrast so sharply with the approach fostered by social media. The marketers and social media influencers would have you believe that likeability is all about following these rules:

- Gather as many likes, subscribes, clicks, and reactions as possible (quality irrelevant)
- Seek to convey an idealized image of yourself, and invite comparison and competition
- Strive for independence, material wealth, self-promotion, influence, and superficial visual appeal
- Finally, if you want to be healthy, then that's all about weight loss, nailing it at the gym, staying young, and optimizing your diet and lifestyle (other human beings not necessary!)

Denworth's book is fascinating in that it gives hard empirical evidence for what most of us already know to be true: **a life centered on quality human connection is a happier and healthier life**.

And yet so many of us allow our ideas about our social lives to be completely shaped and influenced by media and online content that reflects the opposite!

Time to adjust our expectations a little:

- **"I'm a loser who doesn't have enough friends."** Don't worry too much about *how many* friends you have. It's not a competition! Instead focus on the quality and character of those connections, and work on your ability to create and sustain genuine closeness with others.

- **"I have to work on myself before people will like me."** Let go of the idea of becoming some new and improved version of yourself first, before seeking out connection to others. You are actually more likely to connect as the individual and uniquely flawed human being you actually are, right now.
- **"Everyone else finds socializing easier than I do."** Be proactive. You may need to "go first" and instigate vulnerability (by revealing a little of yourself or opening up emotionally) or make time to be with people and prioritize them in your life. It takes effort, patience, and courage, and it won't happen by accident.
- **"I'm missing out."** Finally, are you noticing that social media has made socializing feel stressful, exhausting, isolating, or depressing? It might be time to seek out more real-world connections that focus on authenticity and connection, rather than the mere performance of it!

Action step: Today, think about an expectation you hold about how you "should" be doing socially, and get curious—where did this idea come from? Is it true? Is it useful?

Understanding the "liking gap"

Picture this. You have a conversation with a fairly new acquaintance, and you chat easily enough with them. You find them interesting and likeable, and you try your best to listen, to smile, to ask interesting questions.

Later that day, though, you start to mull over things...

Did you talk too much?

Could you have accidentally offended them?

Why did you have to say that stupid thing you said!?

Without even realizing you're doing it, you might quietly come to the conclusion, "They don't like me very much."

Here's the funny thing: The other person might have come to precisely the same conclusion.

Even funnier still: You both would have been completely wrong!

Boothby et al. (2014) have explored this phenomenon and call it "The Liking Gap." It's a real cognitive bias where **people reliably underestimate how much others like them after a social interaction.**

Several studies were put together to investigate this quirk. The most straightforward went like this:

- Research participants were paired and asked to participate in either casual or more structured conversations with one another.

- They were then each asked to rate how much they liked the other person, and how much they guessed the other person liked *them.*
- The real scores and the actual scores were compared.

The results were notable: **People consistently believed that they had come across worse than they actually did**—at least according to the people they were talking to!

This effect was observed across different conversation types and contexts, and found to be stable even over time. In other words, you could still detect this effect in long established and successful friendships.

What we are looking at is a stable cognitive bias—and it's good news because it means we have solid evidence that **people probably like us more than we think.**

How can we explain this effect? It's possible that…

- Our tiny flaws or social gaffes are just not as noticeable to others as they are to us.
- People do notice them, but are more compassionate, kind, or forgiving than we give them credit for.
- People are simply too absorbed in their own social anxiety to focus on ours!

Putting this insight into practice is more about what you don't do: The next time you leave a social situation, notice your own inner dialogue and *consciously choose to push back against assumptions that others don't like you.*

Is it possible that people occasionally do think badly of us? Sure. The study found that *on average* people were rated more likeable than they guessed, but of course that can include a few ratings that were accurate or even worse than predicted.

Nevertheless, we stand to reduce our own anxiety and boost our confidence even if the most we can say is, "I don't really know what they think of me." Choosing not to assume the worst also means you're not sabotaging the possibility of future connection.

This leads us to an important related concept...

Consider: How might you behave towards someone who you knew disliked you? (In other words, how might you behave if you believed your own assessment that "they don't like me"?).

If you genuinely expected someone to be rude, judgmental, unkind, or disagreeable towards you, how might that change the way you interacted with them?

And how might your behavior towards them change the way they behaved towards you?

If you're thinking that sounds like a self-fulfilling prophecy, then you're right. Tice et al. (1995) wrote about a tendency they call "behavioral confirmation."

Simply, **people tend to behave in ways that confirm other people's expectations of them.**

It's a simple concept, but it has profound implications.

If people expect to receive friendliness from another person, for example, that other person tends to pick up on that expectation, *and fulfil it*. They act friendly, and the prophecy is fulfilled.

We're going to explore the intricacies of behavioral confirmation in a later chapter, but for now, let's combine the liking gap bias *and* the phenomenon of behavioral confirmation:

- **If you believe that people don't really like you**, then you may hold an *expectation* that they will treat you with coldness, and lack of care or kindness.
    - People may unconsciously pick up on this, and through behavioral confirmation, actually come to treat you that way.
    - Combined with the fact that they too might assume that *you* don't like *them*, you may inadvertently confirm their negative expectations.
    - Result: Feelings of disconnection, awkwardness, and even defensiveness.

- **If you believe that people like you**, then you may hold onto the *expectation* that they will treat you with warmth, interest, respect, and kindness.
    - Again, people pick up on your unspoken expectations and validate them, confirming your expectation by behaving as though they do like you.
    - Result: Feelings of connection and bonding.

Act as if people *already* like you, and it will become a self-fulfilling prophecy.

Action step: Assume people like you. Expect it. Then act accordingly.

Tip 1: When you're feeling anxious in a new social situation, try to imagine that the other people are already your friends. Imagine that you've already gone through the vetting process, you already know that they like you, and you already know that you like them.

Tip 2: If this is difficult to imagine, try to first imagine how you feel around your closest and most trusted friends. Then try to imagine transplanting that state of mind into this new situation.

Alternatively, try to recall some of the kind things people have said about you in the past, then meditate on those warm, happy feelings before you go into any social situation. You might be surprised at just how quickly people respond!

Tip 3: In your social group, make a habit of "nice gossiping." Deliberately say flattering things about people to others in their absence, even outright saying how much you like them. Word *will* find its way to the person in question, and the effect on them can be magical.

Self-fulfilling social perceptions

So, now we know that our social beliefs about ourselves matter, and we know that people behave in ways that confirm other people's expectations of them.

This is such a powerful idea that it's worth digging into a little deeper. A clever study by Snyder, Tanke, & Berscheid (1977) was able to neatly demonstrate what they called "self-fulfilling social stereotypes" in a lab setting.

Here's what they did:

- Male research participants were told that they'd be having a telephone conversation with a woman.
- To prepare, they were shown a photo and told it was the woman they'd be speaking to. The trick? It wasn't her:
    - Half the participants were shown a photo of an *unattractive woman*
    - The other half were shown a photo of an *attractive woman*

- The researchers watched closely how both the man and the woman navigated the conversation, in both groups.

Can you predict what they found?

When the men believed that they were speaking to an attractive woman, they behaved accordingly.

→ They treated her with warmth, friendliness, and positivity.

This finding (though perhaps a little depressing) is not entirely unexpected.

The more interesting thing is the way the *woman* responded to this treatment. Being unaware that the man had seen the attractive photo, she behaved in ways that confirmed his expectation of her as attractive.

Read that again: when the woman was treated as an attractive woman, she behaved as an attractive woman, even without conscious awareness of what was happening.

→ The woman acted friendly, confident, and sociable.

You can probably guess what happened in the "unattractive photo" group.

The man expected that the woman on the other end of the line was unattractive, so he treated her as such. She in turn responded with less friendliness, and less engagement.

Two fascinating things are happening here:

- Our expectations about other people can change the way they behave.
- The way other people behave in response can actually confirm our original expectations.

Men's expectations influence their behavior which influences women's behavior which confirms men's expectations—**it's not just a self-fulfilling prophecy, but a reinforcing loop.**

Granted, this research is structured around gender as a variable. Would women behave the same way? What about traits like intelligence or kindness? Could expectations around these traits also lead to self-fulfilling social prophecies?

This particular study doesn't tell us, and it's likely that the study's observed effect is more pronounced than what we'd see in everyday life. Nevertheless, the authors conclude that expectations and social stereotypes can powerfully shape interactions—and **it's a two-way process!**

Perception influences behavior influences perception.

There are some interesting implications here for those of us who'd like to take more conscious control of the way we think, feel, and behave in social situations.

- **Assume the best in others.** Our attitudes and expectations of other people—even if unspoken and unconscious—will impact how we treat them, which in turn will shape their behavior towards us. When you treat people as though they are intelligent, friendly, kind, funny, or appealing, they will often rise to meet that expectation. In other words, **your expectations *create* the very reality you think you're observing.** How amazing is that?!
- **Be attractive. And if you can't be attractive—act as if you are anyway.** Remember that impression formation is a two-way street. Each man in the study initially treated the woman well because she was attractive, but he *continued* to treat her that way because of *her behavior* (friendliness, warmth, positivity).
  - Act like a person who is likeable, and you may find others ready to fulfil that expectation.
  - Paying attention to grooming and appearance is superficial, but it's also an important first step in a process that's more about behavior and attitude. Ever wondered why ordinary-looking people are sometimes seen as wildly attractive?

Yup—actual appearance is only one part of the puzzle!
- **Expect the best.** Humans are social creatures, and they are more influenced by expectation than they know. People unconsciously take their cue from one another, and you can use this to your advantage. *Behave like the person you want to be seen as.*
  o Before a social event, think positively and focus on all the good things you can expect from the interaction. You will behave in ways that unconsciously communicate this to others, who will respond accordingly.
- **You don't *have to* fulfil other people's expectations.** Finally, bear in mind that just because others see you in a certain way, it doesn't mean you have to fulfil that expectation. Stereotypes, prejudices, and assumptions can be unfair and hurtful. But if you're aware of what's happening, you can always choose to consciously act in ways that fit *your* self-identity, regardless of other people's biases:
  o **Not especially attractive?** That doesn't mean you have to act like you're *un*attractive. Hold your head high. Behave "as if."
  o **People not taking you seriously because of your gender, age, size, ethnicity, appearance, social class, or**

whatever? That doesn't mean you can't still convey an attractive aura of self-respect.
- **Is someone convinced you're a bad person when you aren't?** Just because someone has decided who you are and what you're capable of, doesn't mean that this is who you really are. You don't have to play that role. Face unfair accusations with quiet dignity and don't get angry or defensive. Then go on to do whatever it is you know you can do!

Action step: No matter what, people respond to the energy you give off in social interactions. Be positive, expect good things from both yourself and others, and you'll be surprised by how often reality rises to meet you! In your next social interaction, experiment with presenting yourself "as if" you were the person you want others to perceive you to be. Then notice what happens.

Chapter 2: Playing the social game

Social learning and popularity

You've probably been given the advice before: "Just be yourself!"

While this is true, there's actually a little more to it.

A 2011 paper explores how what people find attractive can actually be influenced by watching others—the so-called **social learning theory** (Little et. al., *Social Learning and Human Mate Preferences*).

While beauty may be in the eye of the beholder, we are not always exclusively the ones who decide what we find appealing. **People's tastes have been shown to be influenced by seeing what other people like.**

The idea is that because humans are social beings, they learn from one another. They don't just learn culture and language, but also things like:

- What counts as a high status, likable person

- Who is considered a "catch"
- What's broadly in fashion
- What traits, looks, and attributes are popular

The study found that many animal species display mate-choice copying—i.e., they copy the mate choices of those around them. And while it may not be a flattering reality, humans do it, too!

This kind of mimicry can be thought of as a kind of *social shortcut.*

The authors find, for example, that:

- If someone popular or high-status shows interest in someone, that person appears more attractive to others.
- "Social learning not only influences the attractiveness of specific individuals, but can also generalize to judgements of previously unseen individuals possessing similar physical traits." In other words, the effect holds even for people you haven't met yet.
- Entire groups can start to collectively share the same ideas about what is considered valuable or attractive—this may explain why there can be such big differences between cultures when it comes to who is considered popular.

Now, what are we to make of such findings?

To cut to the chase, we need to understand that **status matters.** And like it or not, status is about what *other people* think.

Without even realizing that they're doing it, people tend to adopt the preferences of those who seem influential, high-status, or respected.

While some might find this truth a little discouraging, there is a notable upside: It means that **you have more control over how you're perceived than you realize.**

While the paper focused more on physical traits and mate value in the dating market, the truth is that human beings take their cue from influential others on all sorts of topics—otherwise there would be no such thing as celebrity brand endorsement or famous musicians sharing their opinions about politics!

We can use this quirk of human social interaction *to our advantage*. Here are some ideas:

- **Pay attention to what people in your social group find attractive or appealing in general.**
    - It's not about blind mimicry. Just be aware, be strategic, and position yourself accordingly.
- **In new social situations, try to win the favor of whoever seems highest status.**
    - You will be perceived as more likeable if you are seen to be approved by others—especially high-status individuals.

- Notice who is succeeding socially around you and try to gently emulate their behaviors and attitude.
- **Spend time in group settings where your positive traits can be observed by others**.
  - If you're dating someone new, consider introducing them to your social circle early on. Them seeing you in a socially validated setting can increase their attraction for you.
  - Allow others to see you receiving praise or approval from others—perhaps at work, or while doing something you're good at.
- **Be careful about automatically positioning yourself as a rebel.**
  - Being strenuously countercultural or pushing hard against the general sentiment of a group may feel harmless or even fun, but it also risks backfiring. People are quick to identify those they unconsciously see as social outcasts, and may just lazily write you off—even if it is unfair!
  - There is nothing wrong or inauthentic about deliberately cultivating traits and qualities that your general community finds worthy. We are social animals, and our behavior is communication. Being popular is not just for high school kids. It's an ancient

social signal, *"I fit in here. I'm valuable. I'm strong and healthy."*

Many of these ideas can sit uncomfortably for people. It can feel inauthentic to try to boost our own social value this way. However, bear in mind a few things:

- **This is not prescriptive, but descriptive** – like it or not, people really do behave this way, including us! If it's going to happen, we might as well understand why and make the best possible use of that knowledge.
- **Social learning mostly applies to superficial physical traits and general trends**– it's a way to get *new* social situations off to the right start and show yourself in the most flattering light possible. It's not a long-term strategy for deep, meaningful relationships.
- **Being conscious and intentional about how you are perceived is not deceptive.** Try not to blindly follow social trends, but ask, "What does this popular preference look like when expressed by *me*?" You are not changing who you really are, just playing around with the frame you use to present yourself—so that people can see and appreciate the real you.

Action step: Think of something that your general social group values or considers high status. *Without faking it*, can you think of a natural way to showcase, highlight, or draw attention to that value in yourself?

Alternatively, think of a person who you know is well-liked and admired. Can you identify one behavior, attitude, or habit they possess that you can start to emulate in your own life? Again—the goal is not to be inauthentic, but to ask, "What does my version of this well-liked thing look like?"

What makes a person popular?

In an interesting paper title "Popularity: Beauty, Intelligence, or Personality?" Fronzetti Colladon et. al. (2021) investigated exactly what it is that makes certain people so well-liked and well-known.

Their study included 200 college students as research participants (do with that information what you will!) and in particular explored the difference between two types of social networks:

1. **Friendship networks** – who people choose to become friends with
2. **Advice networks** – who people choose to go to for help and advice

More specifically, how do people decide which group a friend belongs to, and what personality traits do they possess?

The research team took a closer look at the following traits:

- General personality
- Creativity
- Intelligence
- Energy
- Physical attractiveness / beauty

Are you ready to hear the results? They're not pretty—or rather, pretty is exactly what they are! The researchers found that **physical attractiveness matters most**, i.e., those students who were seen as more physically attractive were also appraised as being good friendship material.

In addition, the researchers conclude that when it comes to advice networks, people had a tendency to value intelligence and creativity more—for obvious reasons.

What can we do with these (perhaps dispiriting) findings?

- **It's *perceived*, not *actual* traits that matter.** Not attractive? Not creative or intelligent? It might not matter that much. If others broadly *perceive* you to be these things—and observe others perceiving you in that way—then you may find yourself ranked accordingly.
    - **Pay attention to grooming, posture, and hygiene.** There's no point telling

yourself these things don't matter. They don't. *And yet they do.* If you play up your strong features, stand tall, smell nice, and show pride in your appearance, you're more likely to register as generally attractive.
- **Consider the impression you're making.** Others tend not to perceive us according to *our* traits, but *their* needs. Without getting too philosophical, it's worth remembering that ultimately, people seek out friendships as a way to meet their underlying needs, not ours. That means we need to consciously consider what they value, and whether they can perceive that value in us.
  - **"Attractive" applies to so much more than physical appearance.** Ask yourself honestly: Are you *appealing* to others? Do you look like someone who adds value to any social situation?
  - **See yourself through other people's eyes.** Take a few pictures or film yourself, then with neutral, objective eyes carefully consider the impression you're giving. Would you be friends with you? Why or why not? Enhance what's working and downplay what isn't.
  - **Project yourself.** You might genuinely be intelligent, but do you *appear* intelligent? You might be good fun, or

kind, or creative—but can people actually *see* that about you, at a glance?

While the study findings may feel discouraging, the truth is that human beings have no other way to quickly assess one another *except* through physical appearance. Natural physical attractiveness certainly exists, but there's more wiggle room than you think——for most people, **average + deliberate effort in grooming = attractive.**

We all have the opportunity to make an amazing impression within the first few split seconds of any social interaction. Do you possess true inner beauty and a lovable character? Then allow people to *see* that by visibly showing yourself to your best advantage.

Don't be down on yourself

Though our book is not specifically about dating, the following study does reveal some interesting insights into the way human beings tend to rank and rate one another... and consequently, how they rank and rate themselves!

Researchers investigating *social comparisons* and *self-perception* (Castro et. al., 2014) conducted an interesting experiment:

- They asked 225 undergraduates to rate themselves on various traits: attractiveness, friendliness, health, ambition, etc.

- About a month later, they asked the participants to view fake "profiles" of people of their own gender, which varied on physical, social, and status-related attributes. They were asked—*how desirable do you think these people would be to the opposite sex?*
- Then the researchers asked them to self-rate (again) their own "mate value"—i.e., to say how valuable they thought they were in the eyes of others—according to the same attributes.
- Finally, they were asked to state what they themselves wanted in a romantic partner.

The findings were fascinating.

People's original self-ratings tended to change once they had seen the fake profiles.

Both men and women's self-perception seems to be influenced by how they see others. In other words, people decide how much "value" they have by appraising the value of those around them.

Overall, seeing people who were less attractive, ambitious, or lower status tended to make people feel better about themselves, whereas viewing people who appeared superior in any way tended to make people feel worse (more on this in the next section).

Yet—and this is the interesting part—exposure to others didn't significantly change what people themselves wanted in a partner.

Think about this for a second.

Seeing the "competition" out there in the world can lower our confidence and feelings of self-worth, even as we maintain fairly realistic expectations of others!

We all seem to intuitively assume what traits the opposite sex tends to value in partners (e.g., men value attractiveness, women value status) and rank ourselves accordingly, assuming that others will rank us in the same way. And yet *our own* mate preferences tend to be fairly stable and not influenced by such rankings and comparisons.

It's funny: we might think "she's beautiful, men will probably love her" or "he's such an alpha male, I bet the girls all want him" and yet we ourselves will have far more nuanced, sophisticated, and forgiving preferences when it comes to the people we are attracted to.

A woman might look at other beautiful and impressive women on social media, compare herself to them, and decide she's inferior. She might think, "Those are really desirable women. I'm not as good as them."

She feels less confident.

Less sure of herself.

More insecure and lacking in self-worth.

Ouch!

On the other hand, a man might be looking at similar social media images and seeing impressive, high-status men. He compares himself to them, feels awful, and quietly decides, "I'm nothing like them. Women want *that* and I don't have it."

He feels awful.

Like he's sub-par.

His self-esteem is on the floor.

Again—ouch!

The ridiculous thing? Both this man and this woman may actually find one another *perfectly matched* and feel seriously attracted to one another!

Social comparison affects your self-perception... but not your own social choices.

While this study focused on comparison and self-perception in the dating market, it can tell us something very interesting about social interaction more broadly.

Comparison to other people can change how we see ourselves, but we need to remember that people's preferences and their perception of *us*—i.e., the things we're actually interested in—largely remains stable.

How does any of this apply to non-romantic relationships?

Well, have you ever felt that other people were more…

- Interesting
- Likeable
- Well-connected
- Sociable
- Popular
- Cool
- Outgoing

…than you? Have you ever thought, "*That's* the kind of person people like, and I'm not like that."?

If you have, you may have been guilty of your own version of **social comparison**.

As we saw in the last chapter, social media is gasoline on the fire of this kind of insecurity, just like marketing, media, and advertising. These things create the illusion of a breezy world where everyone is confident, well-connected, and living their best lives with dozens of good-looking friends…

But it's not real!

Comparing yourself to this illusion will only make you feel bad about yourself and give you a distorted perception of your value to others.

The beautiful people on screens do not even remotely represent the normal range of human attributes, so comparing yourself to them will invariably leave you (mistakenly!) feeling that you're in the bottom 10%.

Even worse—it may make you avoid putting yourself out there, which really *will* shrink your social world and lower your confidence (recall the self-fulfilling social prophecy).

The truth is more comforting: There are people out there in the world who feel *exactly* the way you do about socializing. Even those who appear to be natural-born social butterflies can struggle with loneliness, feelings of inferiority, or awkwardness around others.

What's more, although we're all aware of the social ideal, in the real world there are all sorts of different people out there, who are drawn to all sorts of other different people. And you're one of them!

The takeaways here?

- Be careful with social comparison—it won't support a healthy or realistic long-term self-perception.

- Stay away from social media or other triggers that make you want to retreat or give up.
- Drop the competitive mindset.
- Stop telling yourself that you are uniquely bad at socializing, or that you're inferior to others.
- Shift the focus; stop asking, "How do I compare to others?" and instead ask, "Who am I? What do I want to do? What's interesting? Who do I like?"

Action step: Today, think about what you ordinarily consider your worst or least desirable trait. Can you celebrate that quality today? There is someone out there who thinks that trait is *amazing*. Where might you find them?

Be careful with social comparisons

Let's dig a little deeper into the question of comparison.

Who are you?

And, *how do you know* you're like this?

Long before Castro and colleagues conducted their comparison research, American social psychologist Leon Festinger put forward his Social Comparison Theory in the 1950s. The theory posits that people understand who they are *in context*, i.e., by comparing themselves against others.

Festinger posited that people rank and rate their own position in reality by checking to see how they fare compared to others around them—and this is especially true when there are no objective standards against which to measure oneself.

Self-evaluation, then, is social, and its mechanism is comparison.

We're told that "comparison is the thief of joy" but Festinger claims that for human beings, comparison is really the only way we can evaluate ourselves.

Are you good, attractive, successful, likeable, or talented?

Are your opinions correct?

Are you normal or a bit strange?

Well, you can't answer that unless you know *compared to what*!

There are two types of comparison:

- *Upward* – comparing yourself to those who are perceived as higher up or better off
- *Downward* – comparing yourself to those who are perceived as lower down or worse off

Festinger found that upward and downward comparisons arise from slightly different motivations and produced slightly different outcomes.

Upward social comparison

- Pros: Can act as a powerful source of motivation and inspiration
- Cons: Can create feelings of inferiority and inadequacy

Downward social comparison

- Pros: Can increase self-esteem, provide reassurance, contentment, and validation
- Cons: Can lead to a false sense of superiority or achievement, not to mention dampen empathy

Festinger's contribution was to acknowledge that social comparisons are normal and genuinely useful, leading to accurate social assessment and identity. However, the kind of comparisons we make and the effect they have on our lives matters, too.

But Festinger went further: **Your social group has a direct and powerful influence on the way you see yourself.**

But then… what *is* your social group?

If our sense of self, worldview, mood, self-esteem, identity, and overall satisfaction with life is influenced by social comparison, then we need to be careful about who we're comparing ourselves to.

So, social comparisons are normal, but the outcome of that comparison depends on:

- The kind of comparisons we're making
- The social group we're comparing ourselves against

What kinds of social comparisons are best?

Aspinwall and Taylor (1993) found that **upward comparison is beneficial when people already have a high degree of self-esteem.** When you feel good about yourself, seeing others succeed and excel gives you hope and inspires you to do the same.

However, if your self-esteem is low, if you're feeling insecure or as though your sense of resilience or competence has taken a knock, then upward comparisons can really hurt. They're likely to dampen motivation and crush hope.

Instead, **when you're feeling low, downward social comparisons can have a better effect and provide a little comfort that you're not doing as badly as others!** Downward social comparisons might not always be kind, but they can boost mood, create feelings of gratitude and thankfulness, and drum up a bit of motivation to do better in life.

If you want to feel more motivation and hope, consider your current state of self-esteem:

Feeling good? Compare yourself to those doing a little better.

Feeling low? Compare yourself to those doing worse pro tip: That person could be a past version of yourself!)

And that brings us to the next point: The modern world has desperately distorted and reshaped what most of us consider our social context. In the past, only the people who were literally in our vicinity could be considered part of our social circle, whereas now, technology has made it possible for us to access the images, ideologies, and stories of people we would never have otherwise considered neighbors.

Be mindful:

- **If you're feeling bad about yourself, avoid social media that will only make you feel worse.** Even genuinely successful people can't measure up to those images of wealth, beauty, and luxury. Think of advertising, marketing, and social media as tools for *amplifying* comparison of both kinds.
- **Pay close attention to who you consider your peers.** There is more flexibility today than ever before in how you identify, and the groups you want to belong to—social, political, religious, ideological.
    - You may feel successful and accomplished relative to a low-achieving group, but be honest if you

need to push yourself and seek out mentors and high achieving role models, too.
- You may feel inadequate compared to your current social group, but be realistic and ask whether this is a genuine reflection of your worth, or whether you may need to find a better-aligned "tribe."

- **Find balance.** The ideal social environment is one where you feel like you belong and are accepted, and yet you also feel comfortably challenged to aspire to good things.
  - Be competent, but leave room for other people to shine, too.
  - Find friends and acquaintances who are complementary—you may excel in one area, while they excel in another. You can mutually support one another's growth without resorting to comparison and competition.

- **Work on your self-esteem first.** Sometimes, feelings of low self-worth are simply cognitive distortions and have nothing to do with reality. If this sounds like you, comparison of any kind is not going to help you gain a healthier and more accurate self-perception. Competition is likely to be felt as threat.
  - Instead, work on feelings of intrinsic self-worth and then use *moderate*

upward social comparison to inspire you to aim for more.

Action step: Ask yourself honestly who your current social group is, and how they are shaping the way you see yourself. Is there anything that needs to change?

Be real... but mindful of your presentation

Today, advice to be *authentic* is everywhere. We are told that the primary social ill is that we don't love ourselves enough, just as we are, and that we are entitled to other people's liking and acceptance.

Should we be "authentic"?

Or should we pay careful attention to presenting ourselves in just the right way?

The answer is... yes.

As with most things concerning human beings, there are nuances. Socially successful people have mastered the art of being authentic *and* presenting themselves in a flattering light.

Leary and colleagues (1986) compiled a comprehensive paper about just this topic, titled, "Self-Presentation Tactics and Social Acceptance."

According to Leary et. al., most people do make active use of **self-presentation tactics**, where these are defined as **deliberately attempting to control the way others perceive you.**

We all want to be seen as likeable, competent, kind, etc. We all want to be socially accepted. And regardless of what they say, people have been shown to use a range of techniques to influence others to do just that, including:

- **Ingratiation** – for example flattery, compliments, agreement
- **Self-promotion** – showcasing your skills and competence
- **Exemplification** – trying to show yourself as morally worthy
- **Supplication** – highlighting your own weaknesses to gain sympathy and approval
- **Intimidation** – highlighting your strength so as to appear powerful or dangerous

The technique you choose depends on

- Your social aims
- The context you find yourself in
- Your audience

Do you want to be respected by your rivals and competitors? Maybe exemplification is your frame of choice, with a little light intimidation sprinkled on top.

Do you want to be loved and cherished by a partner? It may be that ingratiation and supplication work best.

Do you want to impress at a job interview? It's self-promotion all the way.

A few points given by Leary et. al.:

- Self-presentation is a normal and essential part of a well-functioning social life. It's not fakery. It's not manipulation. It's strategic *framing*.
- People who subtly align themselves with others are almost always seen as more likeable than those who try to *force* alignment, or those that simply dominate and bulldoze others.
- In general, if you want to be perceived as likeable, then **light ingratiation is your best bet**. This may be indistinguishable from good manners, politeness, etiquette, and being a good conversationalist.

What does it mean to be *ingratiating*?

The good: Attempting to find favor with someone, to win them over, to charm them, get in their good books and flatter them.

The bad: Sucking up, fawning, pandering, groveling, etc.

The ugly: Obsequiousness, boot-licking, and, well brown-nosing.

Done right, ingratiation is like putting on a nice, clean outfit before you attend an important event. Done wrong, it's like wearing a "Kick me" sign on your back.

How do you find the right balance?

It all depends on your goals, context, and audience.

One good rule of thumb: Think about finding *shared vibes*, rather than forcing agreement or liking.

This way, you take charge of your self-presentation and the impression you give, but without being inauthentic.

- Don't be a try hard.
- Listen carefully for natural points of alignment, then lean into those. What priorities, goals or values do you share? Focus on those.
- Echo their enthusiasm, give genuine compliments, be polite, and ask thoughtful questions.
- Smile, use open body language, and pay attention to making others feel seen, heard, and valued.
- Let go of the need to *impress*. Instead, focus on building up good energy and conversational flow.

Action tip: The next time you're in a social situation, consciously adopt this mindset: "This person already likes me. I just have to present myself in such a way that makes it easier for them to recognize that fact."

No fakery, no manipulation, just making yourself easy to appreciate.

Chapter 3: Getting in sync

Facial expressivity and social success

Thinking of getting some Botox? You might want to reconsider.

In an interesting new study (Kavanagh, Whitehouse & Waller, 2024), researchers found evidence for what most of us have intuitively known all along: When it comes to conversation, it's really your facial expression that says the first word.

Fifty-two participants were asked to take part in a video call with another person, and chat through different scenarios. Meanwhile, their facial expressions were being recorded and analyzed according to a Facial Action Coding System (FACS), to objectively measure their facial expressivity.

The recordings were then shown to 176 different participants, who were asked to say how...

- Expressive

- Understandable ("readable")
- Likeable

...they felt the person was.

A second study looked at 1315 participants and their unscripted video chats, and the participants also received a personality test. The video recordings were again analyzed scientifically, and separate participants were asked what they thought of these people, given what they had seen in the recordings.

In both studies, the results were pretty clear: **More facially expressive people were rated as more likeable and "readable" than those who were less expressive.**

But there was more. The researchers also found that:

- Though facial expressivity does vary between people, this trait does appear to be a fixed trait in individuals, and stable across contexts and conversation partners.
- Facial expressivity does appear to correlate with certain personality traits:
  - Agreeableness
  - Extraversion
  - Neuroticism
- Facial expressivity is also associated with better social outcomes, for example during negotiations and conflict resolution (where

both *expressivity* and *agreeableness* tend to predict the best outcomes).

OK, so we know that having a more expressive face makes others perceive you as more likeable, and this translates to being more socially effective.

But facial expressivity is also a stable trait… so does that mean that if we're not naturally expressive, we're doomed?

No!

While dynamic and animated facial expression is a social asset, it doesn't mean that the rest of us can't *consciously* choose to cultivate this part of our social repertoire.

- **Be more aware of how you're using your face**. Pay attention to this aspect of your communication. It may feel a little unnatural at first, but deliberately make your facial movements and expressions more exaggerated:
    o Raise your eyebrows to signal enjoyment, surprise, and interest.
    o Smile and laugh.
    o Nod to signal assent or use head tilts and other gestures to show that you're paying attention and responding to what you hear.
    o Mirror the other person's expressions to signal your active, engaged listening.

- Be dynamic. Allow your expression to change and shift according to the flow of the conversation.
- **Practice!** If you often find that you have a grumpy "neutral" face that doesn't actually reflect how you're feeling, realize that you can change it.
  - Literally rehearse arranging your facial muscles into a comfortable but pleasant expression. This doesn't always come easily or naturally!
  - Before socializing, warm up a little. Like an actor before a performance, run through some facial expressions and practice a few expressive reactions in a mirror. It *will* feel silly, but it will wake your face up and remind your brain to not just *feel* emotions, but *communicate* them outwardly, so others can more easily connect with you.
- **Get feedback.** Facial expressivity can be a big problem for some of us. If this is an issue for you, relax, there's a lot you can do:
  - Play a video of a person speaking and record your face as you listen and react to that person. Watch the video of your own facial expression and take notes. What do you see? How would you feel if someone responded to you in this way? Are your true feelings properly expressed?
  - If possible, get a close and trusted friend to give you some pointers, or practice

subtly being more expressive and observing the response you get.
- **Don't hold back!** Sometimes, anxiety, politeness or uncertainty can make us dampen down our natural responses and "play it cool." Big mistake! Be "readable." Let people see that you're responsive, paying attention, and reacting to what they're sharing. It will make you seem present, engaged, and available.

Being introverted or socially awkward can occasionally make people *turn inward* in social situations. If this sounds like you, it's simply a question of recognizing this and choosing to deliberately *turn outwards* again.

Don't assume that people automatically know what you mean or what you're thinking or feeling—**show them**.

Action step: During your next social interaction, pay close attention to the other person's face. See if can spot little flutters of expression—a raised eye, a slight smile. Then copy it. Not only will this remind you to be more expressive, but you will be perceived as more in sync and engaged.

Send good vibes by smiling

We all know that smiling is a good thing to do in social situations, but have you ever wondered *why*?

What is it about curling up the corners of your mouth or showing your teeth that makes social interactions feel so much nicer?

Well, the answer may lie in the brain's **mirror neurons. These are neurons in the brain that fire when we see another person performing a certain action.**

Think about the last time you...

- Watched a baby's animated face as it laughed or giggled
- Watched a movie where the main character experienced something strange, terrifying, or gross
- Listened as a loved one tearfully told you a sad story

Chances are, your empathy in each of these situations was a real, physical thing—you felt yourself laughing, you unconsciously recoiled or shuddered, or you found yourself unintentionally tearing up, too.

This is the magic of mirror neurons!

Because of mirror neurons, smiling is—in a very real way—neurologically contagious.

Mirror neurons were first discovered in the 80s and 90s (Giacomo Rizzolatti, 1992, 1996) when researchers discovered that when one monkey performed an action, and another monkey observed it, the corresponding neurons in the second monkey's brain also fired—in much the same way as they would if the monkey had been doing that action itself.

The implications are enormous—especially in our understanding about what empathy actually is.

When we say, "I know what you feel" we may be speaking more literally than we know!

Here's the important bit: mirror neurons activate when people smile. Quite literally, in the prefrontal cortex, the neurons and thus the muscles involved in creating a smile were actually activated during the study. It's not just the emotional recognition of the smile—mirror neurons allow us to *physically* simulate and copy what we're seeing.

This mirroring, in fact, may be precisely the way our brains help us understand what the other person is feeling. By copying their expression in our own bodies, we help ourselves experience what they experience, and make sense of it.

Consider how this plays out:

- You smile at Person A
- Person A sees you smiling
- Person A's mirror neurons for smiling are activated
- A cascade of reactions occurs in their brain—as though they were themselves smiling
- They may even smile back at you

- A reinforcing loop of warmth and liking is created

Other interesting studies have shown that when people are prevented from smiling, they are less empathetic and find it more difficult to recognize or understand another person's happiness (Oberman et. al., 2007). The inability to smile brought about an empathetic lapse in recognizing another person's happiness.

What can we do with this information?

- **Smiling doesn't just make other people feel happier, it makes us feel happier, too.** We smile because we're happy, but it turns out *we also feel happy because we smile.*
  - If you're feeling down or lonely, smile, even if just to yourself. Alternatively, watch videos of happy people—comedy works!
- **Smile before you socialize.** You'll activate good feelings within your own brain and transmit them more easily to others. If you've done a short "smile warm up" before socializing, you'll notice that other people are so much warmer and more receptive to you. Smile at yourself in a mirror to release happy feelings.
- **Always start with a smile.** Here's a secret— a smile can work its magic *even if it's fake.* Consciously begin any social interaction with a big, deliberate smile.

- Those with autism may have impaired mirror neuron function, and find it difficult both to read faces, and to convey their own feelings this way; if this resonates with you, consider "smile practice" with a trusted friend or professional so you feel more comfortable and confident smiling in social situations.

Smiling is one of the easiest and fastest ways to boost social connection and create feelings of empathy and chemistry. It's not just about being polite!

Are you a little shy or self-conscious of your smile? Don't be—socially, it's one of your greatest assets.

Action step: Smile. That's it! At strangers, at loved ones, at work, at home. It doesn't matter. It doesn't matter if it's real or fake—the results will be the same.

Moods are contagious

We've already seen that, through the invisible power of mirror neurons, it is possible to induce positive feelings in others with nothing more than a smile.

In a paper enticingly titled, "Mood contagion: the automatic transfer of mood between persons", Neumann and Strack (2000) asked the question,

is it possible to passively transmit *moods* from one person to another?

Most of us have witnessed firsthand that certain states of mind—good or bad—can "rub off" in the course of social interaction. But is there a way to prove this scientifically? And if we knew a little more about the unconscious mechanisms behind such a mood transfer, could we find a way to make those transfers more consciously?

In one study, participants were told that they would be doing a text comprehension test, then they asked to listen to neutral content that was delivered either with a slightly happy (first group) or slightly sad (second group) tone of voice. When tested later, the first group did in fact measure happier than the second group.

What can we infer? **Mood can be transferred**. Interestingly, the effect:

- Occurred even when the content itself was neutral
- Happened automatically and unconsciously
- Seemed to concern general moods—pleasant and unpleasant—rather than specific emotions like confusion or disgust

This makes this kind of "contagion" different from deliberate empathy and emotional sharing.

What's more, the researchers observed that the participants did not seem inclined to analyze their mood change or interpret it in any way.

They just "caught" it and carried on, perhaps believing their mood change was purely their own.

In a second study, participants were asked to repeat a speech they had heard. The researchers found that when people did this, they seemed to automatically and unconsciously mimic the emotional tone they had heard, even though this was not part of the instruction. Again, when measured later, they showed mood changes that brought their emotional state into closer alignment with the speaker's.

Human beings are emotionally porous.

They're suggestible.

In groups, we find ourselves syncing emotionally, even though the changes we experience never filter up into conscious awareness.

How can we use this concept to our benefit?

- **Be aware.** The emotional environments we expose ourselves to can shape our inner experience, so it's worth paying attention to the moods we might be allowing to influence us.
  - Remember → it's not the content that matters, but the *implicit emotional tone*. That means that the kindest, most positive words can lower our mood if that's the way they're delivered!

- **Be selective.** Do you consistently feel down after spending time with certain people? Watching certain content online? Even listening to a particular audiobook? Consider practicing "emotional hygiene" and avoid spending too much time in an unhealthy emotional atmosphere.
- **Take charge.** The "vibe" of any social interaction is not just some random thing that happens; it's often just an average of the different moods that people are contributing. Do your part by conveying warmth, positivity, and relaxation—not in your words, but in your tone:
  - Adopt a warm, gentle tone of voice
  - Smile
  - Use relaxed, open body posture and expansive gestures
  - Make eye contact
  - The easiest way to convey positivity is to genuinely feel it! Before a social event, take the time to get into the right headspace. Your calmness and positivity might not be obvious or ultra-visible, but *people will feel it.*
- **Be strategic.** Sometimes, you might need to persuade or inspire someone, resolve a conflict with them, apologize, teach them, or deliver bad news. These things aren't easy, but you can make them a little easier by subtly modelling the mood state you're

hoping they experience by the time you're done talking.
- **You want to convince people to get excited about your new idea, offer, or plan?** Let your enthusiasm show in your voice.
- **Have you messed up and want your apology to be accepted?** Imagine how you'd speak to someone you were showing compassion and forgiveness to, then use that same tone to apologize.
- **Want to reassure people or help them relax?** There's no use getting stressed out yourself; make your own speech slower, easier, and quieter.

• **Quarantine when necessary!** If you're in a really foul mood, it can be a good idea to put off important social events where possible. It's not that you are required to be perfectly happy before socializing, but rather that you take steps to avoid passing the same "bad mood bug" back and forth amongst your social group!

The main takeaway for our purposes, of course, is simple: if we want to be more successful socially, then we need to stay positive. That positivity will spread, and people will feel better around us.

If people have the unconscious experience, "I'm happy. I feel good. I'm enjoying myself" then it's far easier for them to also think, "I like this person. We're having a good time together."

Action step: Keep a mood diary. Nothing fancy. The more you understand about your own state of mind day to day, the better you'll get at emotional self-regulation, (making minor course corrections to your overall energy moment by moment). This in turn will make you more emotionally aware and socially intelligent.

The chemistry formula

Ah, chemistry.

Few of us would be able to nail down a clear definition… but we all know it when we feel it!

It's somehow just a kind of *spark*.

It's things clicking into place.

It's a flow.

A groove.

Interpersonal chemistry is like being on the same wavelength, or experiencing a kind of alchemy of energies—the whole being magically greater than the sum of the parts.

The thing is, **chemistry is not just a romantic phenomenon**—in fact, if it's an especially successful or satisfying relationship of *any* kind, it usually comes down to chemistry sooner or later.

APS Fellow Harry T. Reis, Annie Regan and Sonja Lyubomirsky recently explored the idea of chemistry as a psychological concept, and published their findings in the journal *Perspectives on Psychological Science* (2021, "Interpersonal chemistry: What is it, how does it emerge, and how does it operate?").

Firstly, they wanted to create a clearer model and definition of chemistry.

The bad news: Chemistry really is spontaneous and can't be forced.

The good news: If we understand more about the characteristics and features of chemistry, we can do a lot to encourage and cultivate it.

The researchers had two questions:

1. What does chemistry look like? (What are its expressed behaviors?)

2. What does chemistry feel like? (The psychological perception of the people experiencing it.)

Let's start with the first one—the way chemistry looks. The study found that chemistry is revealed in the way that people *respond* and *react* to one another:

- There is a sense of being **coordinated and in sync.**
    - They mirror one another's gestures, facial expressions, or language.

- They match one another's tone, rhythm, and pacing.
- They appear to be supporting one another towards a shared goal; there is turn taking, cooperation, and a feeling of shared intent.

This leads directly to the second question—what chemistry *feels* like. Here, the researchers broke the perception of chemistry down into three parts:

- **Cognitive**: The sensation that you and the other person "get" one another and are sharing the same mindset, thoughts, or perspective on things.

- **Emotional**: The sensation of a shared positive emotional experience, be it attraction, liking, warmth, appreciation, humor, empathy, or understanding.

- **Behavioral**: The sensation that you are working well together on a shared goal or coordinated activity.

Did you notice the one word in common for all three? It's **share**.

More than anything, chemistry is a result of a perception of similarity, togetherness, and coordination.

You can't always create that magical feeling from nothing, but what you can do is **gently**

encourage those feelings of sharing, so that chemistry has the greatest chance of developing.

The chemistry formula = The perception that you and another person are *thinking* together, *feeling* (good) together and *acting* together.

How can you consciously create that feeling of alignment?

- **Mirror**—Listen carefully to how they're expressing themselves and reflect it back to them to create an enjoyable feeling of congruence.
    - Use the same language, expressions, metaphors, and verbal idiosyncrasies.
    - Notice their posture and movement and subtly copy it.
    - Pay attention to their voice—the tone, pacing, volume, pitch, articulation, speed, and so on—and match it. This is literally how you "speak their language."
- **Stay in the present.** Chemistry emerges naturally—it cannot be planned, and it's not about fixed traits or first impressions, but about how people interact over time.
    - You cannot build real chemistry online, or through pictures or written messages alone. Seek face-to-face interactions wherever possible. Chemistry grows out of dynamic back-and-forth interactions. It's a living conversation.
    - Matching algorithms on dating platforms cannot accurately predict chemistry.

There's only one way to find out—meet in real life, in real time.
- Chemistry is the feeling that something special, something a little different is happening. You can demonstrate this by paying close, active attention, listening well, and bringing an attitude of genuine respect, gratitude and curiosity.

- **Get out of your head.** Chemistry is non-verbal and embodied. This means that you can easily miss it if you're too caught up in your own thoughts!
  - Pause. Take a deep breath. Come to the moment and let go of any preconceived ideas about where the conversation should go. Be responsive to what is spontaneously unfolding.
  - Create space, then let nature take its course. Instead of trying to control everything, simply pay attention to creating a good space for chemistry to happen. Get rid of distractions, make space, find time, and reduce anxiety levels.

Are you guilty of any of the following chemistry killers?

Arguing or nitpicking. Even if you're right, avoid connection-killing phrases like "well, actually…" or subtly challenging or contradicting the other person. This will only be felt as a rupture of that precious sense of collaboration.

Being overly serious. Chemistry is fun. It feels like play! Being overly literal, judgmental, pessimistic, cautious, superior, or sensitive can get in the way of that enjoyable flow.

Lack of responsiveness. People love to feel seen. To feel heard. To feel *felt* by others. You need to show that you are genuinely receptive and open to the other person. You want to communicate nonverbally: "I am accessible! You have reached me!"

Closed-mindedness. Chemistry has a lot to do with perspective-taking. Show flexibility, empathy, and a willingness to see into other people's worlds. Ask questions. Don't make assumptions.

A few final chemistry-building tricks:

- Use "we" a lot in casual conversation. "Wow, we're good at this, huh?"
- Actively point out similarities and complementarities. "Us crazy dog people have to stick together..."
- If on a first date or hanging out with new friends, suggest an activity that encourages teamwork or mutual play.
- Literally say things like, "I get you", "I understand completely", and "we're on the same page."

Action step: Try your hand at a little (platonic) chemistry creation in your next conversation.

Get in sync and *share the moment*. Make your goal for the interaction to simply create as warm an atmosphere as possible.

Chapter 4: What friendships are made of

Display commonality

As we've seen, chemistry can't be forced or predicted—but it can be encouraged.

Chemistry can be thought of **as a mutual recognition of commonality.**

It's two people simultaneously experiencing the same insight: "Hey, this person is like me."

You like each other... because you're like each other.

In a 2019 paper titled, "Displaying Things in Common to Encourage Friendship Formation: A Large Randomized Field Experiment" (Sun & Taylor, 2019), these ideas are explored more fully.

The authors conducted a randomized field experiment—which simply means that they observed people in their natural online environment. They wanted to see whether showing users information they shared in common with one another made them more likely to actually become friends.

Would you be more likely to connect with someone if you saw they had things in common with you, for example the same hometown, education, work, interests, or music tastes?

According to the study, yes!

The "randomized" part of the study means that as users browsed profiles of people they weren't already friends with, they were either shown a profile as is, or a profile with the shared information highlighted. Then the researchers checked in later to see what friendships, if any, had developed.

The results aren't surprising in the least:

- Those being shown things they had in common with another person were statistically more likely to form friend connections with that person.
- This effect seemed stable across all demographic groups—age, gender, etc.
- Most interestingly, the effect actually seemed greatest for those who didn't have too much in common already. *The more unexpected or surprising a point of commonality, the greater the effect!*

These findings can show us something rather fascinating about how people actually form friendships—versus how we believe they do.

The fact of coming from the same hometown or sharing the same interests *does not* in itself predict a greater chance of friendship. Two strangers could have a mediocre conversation and then go their separate ways without ever realizing that they had something important in common.

This is because it's not the commonality itself, but the fact of *knowing* that you have something in common that seems to create feelings of rapport and shared identity.

It's a subtle but important distinction. It's not commonality that matters, but the recognition of that commonality, and the feeling it inspires.

In fact, the study found that discovering commonality where it was completely unexpected is the most enjoyable of all.

The takeaway? Find something in common with every new person you meet, and do it as soon as possible.

Here are some ideas:

- **Don't be mysterious!** It may be tempting to present yourself in a generic, inoffensive way, but unless you regularly express specific details about yourself, other people won't have the chance to find any common ground with you. Don't be shy. Share facts about yourself, and be forthcoming about your interests and experiences, to uncover points of commonality as soon as possible.

- **Use commonality to ease through friction.** Are you finding it difficult to break the ice with someone? Try to intentionally find something you have in common, and then draw *their* attention to it. Let them see you enjoying the fact that you share something. Keep asking questions and showing interest, then pounce on anything that implies that in at least one way, you are from the same "tribe."

- **Make use of cues and notice other people's cues**. Reveal to others who you are in little ways. Wear your favorite band T-shirt, display a conversation-starting keyring, or randomly drop little hints in conversation that other people can run with. "Must have inherited all these freckles from my Irish grandma!" Similarly, notice when other people are doing this and respond. "You said you were at the lab earlier... I'm curious, what work do you do?"

Action step: One foolproof point of commonality is simply sharing the present moment. For example you're both waiting at a bus stop looking at the same rain, you're both at the same wedding, or you're both glancing at the same newspaper in the supermarket checkout line. So you have something in common! If you want to chat, make a comment about *that*.

If you're really struggling to find something in common, don't worry—it doesn't matter how big and significant the point of similarity is, *only that there is one*. Almost everyone likes puppies, free stuff, and pleasant weather, right? Start there!

What makes people bond?

The human body has evolved to thrive on a particular kind of diet.

In the same way, the human mind has evolved to thrive on a particular type of social interaction.

If we want to know what to eat for good health, we can take inspiration from our prehistoric ancestors' diets, since that diet is precisely what shaped and influenced how our bodies work today.

Well, what type of social interaction has a human being evolved for?

And how can we use that knowledge to, well, make friends and influence people?

Sanchiz et. al. (2016) asked the same question in their paper, "What Makes People Bond?: A Study on Social Interactions and Common Life Points on Facebook."

These researchers analyzed the way people interacted on Facebook. Specifically, they looked at the relationship between users' perceived **connectedness**, their **social interactions**, and what they called **common life points**.

Interestingly, the authors defined "connectedness" as a subjective measure, i.e., it's all about a person's *perception* of being socially bonded to others.

Their main finding:

Homophily played an important role in bonding.

- Homo = same
- Philo = love
- Homophily = loving those that are most similar to ourselves

It's the rule of commonality again!

Human beings have, for most of their history as a species, lived in smallish bands or groups of *similar* people. **We have evolved to bond with those who are similar to ourselves**, often quite literally because we are related to them. Indeed, for human beings, "getting on with my kin" is more or less the definition of what it means to be social.

The study authors found that even in digital spaces like social media, people feel more bonded and connected to those who share "common life points" such as

- Coming from the same town or city
- Having the same education or background
- Doing the same job
- Sharing interests, hobbies, or skills
- Sharing common life experiences

The greater the number of common life points, the greater the sense of perceived bonding and connectedness.

Let's cut to the chase: **Want people to like you? Find a way to send them a clear message: "You and me are the same!"**

A distinction, here. *Commonality* merely describes the state of sharing something, for example you both have twins, you both love Buffy the Vampire Slayer, or you're both vegetarians. It's like recognizing that the word *frog* and *forage* share a lot of the same letters.

However, *homophily* goes a little deeper. It's about recognizing that the other person is of a similar type. As a whole person, they belong in the same category as you, and you like that. You're both introverted, arty types, say. Or you're both anxious high achievers. Homophily is like recognizing the connection between the words *frog* and *toad*. They don't have much in common, but they feel close to being the "same."

This "same" feeling is a shortcut to liking and connection.

A question arises: What if you really aren't anything like them?

Answer: Remember that it's *perceived* similarity that matters.

If you want to connect with people, deliberately find and highlight points of similarity—even if you have to work quite hard to discover them!

The irony is that social anxiety can sometimes make people feel insecure, so they attempt to elevate themselves by highlighting everything that makes them unique or unusual—an attempt that you can now understand will probably backfire.

Similarly, trying to impress others with abstract facts and details means you may miss out on *personal* stories that might reveal interesting point of commonality.

Action step: Every time you meet someone new, quickly search out something you have in common, even if it's superficial. Ask questions to uncover things you might share. Once you find something, shine a little spotlight on it.

The world is no longer limited to our tiny tribe, so of course you may not literally have much in common with another person. But **using the**

language of commonality will trigger feelings of connectedness anyway:

- Use the magic words "us" and "we"
- Throw in phrases like "people like us"
- Show genuine appreciation and joy when you discover a commonality. "I love meeting fellow cyclists!"

Have you stumbled on something that is actually a serious point of difference? Don't dwell on it!

Frequent, low-stakes exposure

So far, we've seen that when it comes to friendships, "birds of a feather flock together"— i.e., commonality and homophily are super important. But it's not all that's important.

Remember how easy it was to make friends in elementary school?

You probably weren't even trying. They were your friends and they were just... there.

Well, one of social psychology's most robust findings is just this insight, and it's called the mere exposure effect.

Mere exposure effect = the phenomenon where people tend to like those who they are simply exposed to most often.

In other words, on an entirely unconscious level, *familiarity* eventually feels like *comfort* and *liking*. You made friends with the school kids who were around you all the time... precisely because they were around you all the time.

The interesting part: The mere exposure effect works even when interactions are superficial. And I mean *really* superficial. A study by Moreland & Beach (1992) showed that female students attending a college class were rated as significantly more likeable than students that didn't attend class as much—even though they never spoke to anyone.

How encouraging is that? Simply seeing a person's face over and over again is enough to have them rate you as more likeable!

The proximity effect = The idea that physically being close to someone supports bonding. It makes sense; people who you encounter in the physical world are more likely to become friends.

Spatial closeness → psychological and social closeness.

People who are familiar and predictably in your environment elicit more trust and liking from us. This certainly explains our elementary school friendships!

It also explains how easily people connect when they frequently spend time together:

- At work
- In dorm rooms or shared residences

- In gyms or other spaces for shared hobbies and sports
- As neighbors or involved community members
- Even the person who works at the coffee shop on your corner!

Zajonc (1968) showed that *repeated exposure* to a stimulus broadly increases our positive feelings towards it, even if that exposure is beneath our conscious awareness. For Zajonc, "stimulus" could mean a word, image, or symbol—which might explain why companies are willing to pay so much money for brand exposure!

Festinger, Schachter, & Back (1950) similarly showed that when it comes to friendship formation, proximity really does matter. By studying student housing at MIT and the emerging friendship patterns on campus, they found that people were more likely to become friends if they lived in adjacent rooms or in rooms in high-traffic areas, where they could be seen.

It's simple—where possible, **make yourself visible!**

Exposure and proximity don't need to be intense or prolonged to have this bonding effect. For this effect to take hold, interaction is not even required—just presence.

All you need is for your exposure to be:
- Low stakes
- Frequent

The implications are clear: If you want to make—and keep—friends, you need to stick around. Literally. Be in people's field of vision. Give them a chance to get familiar with seeing you around the place.

Over time, forming a friendship with you will feel **natural, obvious, and organic**—i.e., you won't have to do too much to get it going.

Friendships take time. The more often you show up, the more presence you bring, the more the exposure and proximity effects can work their magic.

What can we do practically?

- **Become a "regular."** Go to the same places often or sign up to be a regular attender at a gym, sports club, community center, or even a local café. Take the pressure off and make yourself a predictable and familiar presence in a place you like.
- **Don't flake.** Keep showing up and showing your face. If you're pressed for time or not in the mood to socialize, then make an appearance just for a little while. Exposure is about frequency, not duration.

- **Set up little rituals and routines.** Things that are repeated are more believable. Familiarity often leads to preference. Offer frequent, lightweight in-jokes, or have a little "routine" that you go through with people—even if superficial. These little habits actually form the foundation of a possible friendship.
- **Quantity is better than quality.** At least at first! When dating, choose shorter but more frequent dates, and avoid going too long without seeing one another. In fact, you don't always need to make it a "date" at all. Drop by, check in, share a five-minute catch up… these things take barely any time but slowly and surely build trust and affection.
- **Just be around.** Are you on a family WhatsApp group, a work forum, or a Discord server? Are you often in Zoom meetings? Be visible. Post and comment often even if it's just to show your (digital) face and remind people that you're there.

Finally, there is an interesting consequence to the proximity and exposure effect: We need to choose our friends wisely. If merely being around someone makes us tacitly like them more, it's worth paying attention to who we expose ourselves to!

Action step: Take a look at your current day-to-day schedule and the things you do routinely. Is there a way to make one of these things more intrinsically social? For example, if you tend to work out at home, consider joining a gym or signing up for group classes.

Do things together...

In their paper, "A Shared Intentionality Account of Uniquely Human Social Bonding", Wolf & Tomasello (2023) suggest that there is something very unique about the social bonding that humans engage in... they call it **shared intentionality.**

What kind of social interactions have this quality? Well, anything that is based on a mutual and unspoken sense that **"we are in this together."**

While all primates socialize in similar ways, human beings have social networks that are the largest and most complex of all. For us, things like laughter, music, dancing, shared rituals, and collective problem-solving can bring us closely together.

A "triadic" shared experience = one person + another person + a shared object or activity.

For example:

- You're in the kitchen with your mom and she's showing you how to stuff the turkey properly.

- Three friends put their heads together to fix a broken flashlight on a weekend camping trip.
- Two people play chess and gossip.
- A therapist talks her client through a worksheet she did the day before.
- A couple are on a date at the movie theater, and having a cute playfight about what snacks to buy at the kiosk.

Can you see the three parts of the formula in each of the above examples?

According to Wolf & Tomasello, and other related theorists, human bonding is not just about the ability to share emotional states, but also to be conscious that you are sharing them.

In other words: "We are sharing a moment here. I can tell that you can tell that we're sharing a moment here."

Now, for Wolf & Tomasello, their approach has been to merely *describe* human bonding behavior, and what makes it so special. But for our purposes, we can use their findings to reverse-engineer those amazing feelings of closeness. How?

- **Simple—do things together.** To strengthen friendships, choose any activity that you can frame as a shared goal. This includes team sports, hobbies, and recreation, but also everyday

activities. The important thing is that you're actively working *together*—not just side by side.
- **Build awareness around the experience.** The research shows that human beings have a unique capacity for "shared metacognition." Show appreciation for bonding as it's unfolding. Make eye contact. Draw attention to the fact that you're enjoying their company, working together well, or making a good team. "Woah, nice work, you read my mind!"
- **Share the problem-solving process.** Be transparent with your thought process and ask people about theirs. Think aloud, together. An experience doesn't have to be positive or easy to be a shared goal. Many deep friendships have been forged in adversity and struggle because it's not about the experience itself, but that you experienced it *together*.
- **Ask for help.** "Help me pick out a birthday card?" is so much more interesting than just, "Hey, wanna hang out?" Collaborate. Create that "we" moment. Temporarily become a team.
- **Create bonding rituals.** For example, have a regular "Wednesday coffee" where you offload and share plans and goals for the rest of the week, or make a point of always walking home with the same

person after class—here, your shared goal is simply getting home.
- **Avoid "nothing" interactions.** Remember the triad—you, the other person, and *something*. Conversation is great, but for deeper bonding you sometimes need a third thing, a target, or shared intention. This can then act as a trigger for deeper connection. If a coffee date feels a little boring, for example, find the shared intentionality. You might people watch together and have fun making up imaginary stories about their lives. You might dissect the menu together. Whatever it is, do it *together*.

Action step: If socializing sometimes seems intimidating, reframe it for yourself as a normal everyday activity... that you just happen to be sharing with someone else. When befriending new people, a great low-stakes option is just to invite them to hang out with you as you do the things you normally do.

...but screen time doesn't count

According to Wolf & Dotson (2025, "Online Experience Sharing Without Explicit Social Interaction"), watching TV or online videos together does *not* create a feeling of connection.

For Wolf & Dotson's study, participants were put in two groups:

- **Group 1:** The participant watched a video together with a partner (here, "partner" was actually a pre-recorded, silent video of their partner, to ensure there really was no interaction).
- **Group 2:** The participant watched a video alone (i.e., they knew their partner was away doing something unrelated).

In both groups, participants were asked to carefully rate how bonded they felt to their partners, either present or absent. The results? Group 1 and 2 reported identical bonding scores.

Basically, Wolf & Dotson find that watching screens together creates no additional feelings of social connection to a person compared to being completely separate from them. While watching TV together has long been the lazy default way to socialize, the truth is that this so-called **"passive co-viewing" doesn't build real bonds.**

Not explicitly making an effort to talk to one another and interact? Then that simultaneous screen-watching is equivalent to solo screen watching. Fun and relaxing? Maybe. But it won't strengthen social bonds.

While there *have* been some research studies suggesting that in-person "joint attention" does enhance feelings of social connection, Wolf & Dotson's research finds the opposite.

What we can conclude:

Shared online experience is unlikely to produce any meaningful sense of closeness or bonding, no matter how synchronized, simultaneous, or parallel it may be.

The reason will be clear to everyone. Passive co-viewing:

- Does not leverage our innate bonding mechanisms
- Does not allow for emotional or informational exchange
- Does not provide an opportunity for responsiveness or feedback

When it comes down to it, **there are no shortcuts to real, active social engagement.**

Passive digital co-experiences will not deepen connection, nor will watching videos or TV together—unless of course there is an active attempt to bring in dynamic interaction. How?

- Avoid movies as a date option. If you do opt for a movie, make a point of discussing it before or afterwards. Even little comments and interjections mid-movie can turn a merely simultaneous experience into a connected one.
- If you're trying to bond with friends and family who are far away, choose online activities that support conversation and interaction—play a computer game

while chatting or have a meaningful conversation over video chat.
- If you find a funny meme, article, or picture you want to share with a friend, instead of passively sharing it, add some context, an observation, or a question. "Hey, I watched this clip and knew you'd love it. Can you guess which part made me think of you?"

Action step: How much space is passive co-viewing taking up in your calendar? That could be time devoted to creating and strengthening real social bonds. Think of ways to replace it with engaged, connected, and interactive activities—like games, discussions, or group activities.

Bond through shared experiences

A paper published in the *Royal Society Open Science* journal (Chung et. al., 2024) was interested in exploring the exact way that people bond with one another in shared experiences.

We've seen that sharing an experience with someone can help you bond, but these researchers wanted to know more:

What exactly leads to bonding?

Shared experiences seem important, but do people have to feel the same way about these experiences, and at the same time?

Most importantly, does the *intensity* of the emotion matter?

To try and answer these questions, the researchers organized study participants into pairs, with each pair watching one of three possible types of five-minute video:

- Type 1: A comedy (positive emotion)
- Type 2: A documentary about animal cruelty (negative emotion)
- Type 3: Scenes from a library university (neutral emotion)

Some of these pairs watched the film with a curtain between them (so they couldn't actually see their partner), others with no curtain. Then, the researchers measured all sorts of things:

- How connected participants felt to their partner
- How much emotional arousal they experienced
- How much they identified with their partner
- How much they wanted to interact with that partner again in the future

They also measured physiological data (heart rate, skin conductance, etc.) while people watched.

Interested in what they found? The researchers discovered that:

- **Emotional intensity tends to support bonding**, but only in the presence of joint attention (i.e., the pairs could actually see each other).
- **Emotional convergence or synchrony is not necessary**, in other words, the participants felt bonded during shared emotionally intense moments, even if they were feeling completely different emotions! It was the *intensity* of the emotion that seemed to matter, not the *similarity*.
- **Bonding can be purely nonverbal**, meaning that the feeling of shared experience and connection can be created completely without words. Example: eye contact and mirrored facial expressions.
- **Shared emotions bond us—positive or negative.** Emotional intensity appeared to foster bonding and connection, whether it was in response to the depressing documentary or the comedy. It was the boring library movie that produced the weakest bond.

Psychologists have called intense shared emotional experience **collective effervescence.** It's that magical thing that happens when two or more people come together and share an emotional moment, gluing the group more closely together and creating feelings of security, togetherness, and affiliation.

This study suggests that it doesn't matter what the feelings are, and that the people involved don't have to be experiencing the same feelings, nor verbally express them. In fact, a sense of bonding can occur in complete silence, or with nothing more than a few exchanged glances.

What matters most is joint intense emotional arousal. What matters is that people are emotionally engaged, and that they are emotionally engaged *together*.

The question now is, how can we create these kinds of intense, shared emotional experiences in our own lives?

- As we've already seen, "passive co-viewing" fails to promote bonding, but if you watch something together, **choose something emotionally charged.**
  - A powerful or controversial film, a comedy, or a nostalgic classic.
  - As you watch, make eye contact with the other person, share facial expressions, and chip in with comments. Notice their reactions and let them see yours.
- **Attend emotionally stimulating live events.** Does it induce collective joy, inspire awe, or create tension? Then go for it! Think about:
  - Concerts and performances
  - Sports
  - Moving religious services
  - Theater

- Rousing talks, marches, or demonstrations. As you watch, cheer, sing along, comment, react, or gasp in sync to the stimulus—what you're really interacting with is not the show, but the other person.
- **Do meaningful activities together.** Going for coffee is boring. It's neutral. Instead, choose shared activities that make you feel something:
  - Volunteering
  - Fundraising
  - Advocacy or community work
  - Spending time with animals or children
  - Making music or art together
  - Sharing something meaningful—prayer, a sunset walk, a ritual, or a moment in beautiful nature allows for shared feelings of gratitude, wonder, and transcendence. Powerful stuff!
  - The best part? Engage with them while you do the task; reflect together.
- **Leverage fear.** It doesn't matter if an emotion is negative:
  - Go to a theme park and ride rollercoasters or do a bungee jump.
  - Face a challenge or hardship together (that's why triathlons were invented, right?).
- **Leverage sadness.** It may not have occurred to you, but moments of loss, frustration, vulnerability, or disappointment are actually

wonderful opportunities to draw closer to someone.

- ○ Someone crying or upset? Don't rush in to fix everything; just sit and be *with* them. Your presence will not just be a support for them, but a key moment to bond.

Human beings were built to *feel with* one another. Relax, and don't worry too much about creating perfect moments or curated encounters. Remind yourself that humans bond via emotions—*all* emotions. That means that even difficulty, disagreement, or miscommunication is a chance to draw closer connections!

Action step: See if you can schedule an emotion-based experience with a new friend this week. The only limit is your imagination.

Reciprocity matters more than perfection

Physicist, engineer, and systems scientist Erik W. Aslaksen is known for his interdisciplinary work exploring how society evolves as a complex system. In his book, *The Social Bond* (Springer, 2018) he describes how **society itself is a kind of information-processing system.**

Every time individuals in this system interact to form a social bond, they contribute to our societal evolution and nothing less than our collective intelligence as a species. Social interactions between individuals, then, shape and influence this larger information-processing system called society.

Your individual identity, free will, intelligence, and choices (yes, *yours*) all contribute to the shared social bond—and influence its evolutionary course over time.

Aslaksen sees society not just sociologically but uses systems and engineering perspectives to understand how society actually arises and evolves over time. Basically, Aslaksen has made a formal and academic inquiry into what is more casually known as "the fabric of society"

So what keeps this fabric intact?

Aslaksen argues that **what matters most is *interactions* between individuals, not isolated traits or outcomes.**

A social bond—the glue that holds us all together—is based on:

- Frequent, low stakes exposure to one another
- Information exchange, responsiveness, and reciprocal feedback (that's "conversation" to you and me)
- Continuity of connection

For Aslaksen, it's not so much about the nodes in a network (the people themselves), but the connections between those nodes (how they interact).

In other words, people are held together into something called "society" when they interact often and keep on interacting over time. What matters here is the interaction itself—regardless of the correctness of that interaction.

From this perspective, human connection counts as successful not because it's perfect, but because *it happens.* Socializing, in other words, doesn't always have to be harmonious or productive to create strong feelings of connection, trust, and liking.

All that matters is dynamic interaction, i.e., that people engage and respond to each other frequently, creating a feedback loop of mutual influence.

Reciprocity = System Reinforcement

Social bonds are strengthened when there is interaction, engagement, receptivity, responsiveness, and a sense of give-and-take.

Input from one person triggers output in the other.

The loop continues.

The system stabilizes and strengthens.

Voila! We have a *society*.

Aslaksen's focus on *interaction* is a great relief in two big ways:

1. If there is reciprocation, a bond forms, no matter how imperfect the interaction. That means that there is wiggle room in every relationship for friction, disagreement, and misunderstanding.
2. It's not about how interesting, skillful, or persuasive you personally are—it's not about your traits at all, but the quality of the *connection*. This means you can stop worrying about your "performance." After all, even if you were acting "perfectly", if the other person didn't reciprocate and respond, how could a bond form?

When these bonds are taken online, things get confusing. Social media platforms can promulgate the lie that meaningful interaction = perfect outcomes. In other words, we are encouraged to prioritize the perfect *appearance* or *performance* of social engagement… while real connection suffers.

Performative perfection ≠ connection.

Responsive, mutual engagement = lasting connection (even if it's imperfect).

The big takeaways:

- Don't sweat it. interactions don't have to be perfect—"good enough" still gets the job done.

- Focus on reciprocation, dynamic interaction, and that magical back-and-forth. Connection isn't static. It's not a trait. It's alive, and it's a dialogue.
- If you want to make friends, the best thing you can do is consistently demonstrate willingness to respond, reciprocate, adjust, and interact with others. The quality of the interaction is not as important as your ongoing *willingness* to interact.

How can we apply these insights to our own social lives?

- **Can't think of anything interesting to say?** It doesn't matter. Just say something. It might be awkward, but what matters more is the effort towards reciprocity that you've made.

- **Do you feel boring?** That's OK—it's not necessary for you to entertain anyone. Listen, acknowledge what you hear, then ask a small follow up question. You don't need to perform—just find that reciprocal rhythm of back-and-forth.

- **Not "feeling it"?** That's not a big deal. Small check-ins matter more than deep and meaningful conversations, anyway. Things don't have to be amazing all the time. Just keep the thread alive and current. Create little moments of micro-connection that communicate, "I see you, I remember you, I care about you."

- **Has the vibe gone a little weird?** Rest assured that there is room for imperfection, lulls, disagreements, awkwardness, distance, or even outright conflict. What's important is what you do next. Remember that it's reciprocity that reinforces the system, not necessarily agreement.

Action step: Consistently showing up socially is like putting in reps in the gym: small, consistent effort always matters more than dramatic, one-and-done action. Today, think of a relationship that feels a little neglected or stagnant, and commit to showing that person your willingness to keep the interaction going. Reach out, send a message, invite them somewhere or give them a call. Your gesture doesn't have to be big and it doesn't have to be perfect. Just make it.

Chapter 5: Tools of the trade

Why first impressions matter

We all know that first impressions count, but there may be an aspect to this you have not considered: The order in which you reveal certain pieces of information matters, too.

In a paper titled, "Primacy Effect in Impression Formation" Norman Anderson (1968) concludes that **the information a person shares about themselves first has an outsize influence on the overall impression we form of them.**

Your first interaction with someone is where they make their first impression of you, but it turns out that the things you say *first* have the greatest impact.

Generally, a primacy effect = the tendency to remember the first items in a given list or sequence better than the items in the middle or at the end. We tend to remember—and sometimes *like*—the things we encounter first.

Anderson wanted to see if primacy effects were observable in the way people formed first impressions of one another. They did.

His method was pretty simple:

- Test participants were shown profiles of people they might hypothetically be friends with.
- The same traits were presented to participants; however the *order* of those traits was varied (sometimes the negative traits were first and the positive last, sometimes vice versa etc.).
- Participants were asked in each case to say the first impression they had of this hypothetical person.

Now, even though the participants read the entire list, and even though the lists contained identical items, people on average responded differently according to how the lists were *ordered*.

The traits presented first had a stronger impact on overall impression, i.e., if the first few traits were negative, the overall impression was negative, even if plenty of positive traits followed.

Anderson believes that there is a sort of unconscious "cognitive averaging" phenomenon at play. It's as though the early traits set a "baseline" and this baseline skews or distorts the way the rest of the traits are interpreted. If you read the negative traits first, for example, you might read the positive ones later and unconsciously think, "Well, she's a bad person with a few good traits" rather than the other way around!

Imagine these early traits act almost like a headline, with everything that follows playing the role of supporting statement. **The first things you say about yourself matter because they shape the way the other person will interpret everything you say subsequently.**

Want to make a good first impression? Make those first 30 seconds count and showcase what you feel is your best trait. It may feel a little cheesy, but don't be afraid to literally say things like, "I'm a ___ kind of person." The other person will likely take your word for this and interpret the rest of the conversation in that light.

Action step: Whatever you do, *don't* showcase obviously negative traits first thing. You may just be joking or trying to be ironic, but it will have a negative impact nevertheless, even if you—and the other person—are unconscious of it.

Put in a good word for yourself

Don't you wish that there was a magic word you could say that would instantly have everyone like you?

Well, research by Harold H. Kelley suggests there may actually be such a word ("The Warm-Cold Variable in First Impressions of Persons", 1950).

Actually, Kelley was interested in two words in particular: **warm** and **cold**.

Kelley set out his research in a way not dissimilar to Anderson:

- Student participants were broken into two groups. Both groups were told that they were about to meet a guest lecturer.
- Beforehand, they were primed with a description of this lecturer, and told that he was smart, talented, hard-working etc.
- Both groups were given exactly the same description of the lecturer, with one crucial difference:
    - Group 1 was shown a description that said the lecturer was *warm.*
    - Group 2 was shown a description that said the lecturer was *cold.*
- The students were later asked to rate their overall impression of this lecturer, according to personality traits like likeability, approachability, sociability, etc.

Now, even though the two groups met the very same lecturer, and even though they were primed with a description that was identical in every way *except for that one word*, there were measurable differences in the participants' ratings:

Group 1, the "warm" group, rated the guest lecturer as more sociable, considerate, humane, and humorous than did Group 2, the "cold" group. In fact, the cold group also rated the lecturer as less approachable, more aloof, more serious, and overall less likeable.

All because of one word!

Clearly, the language we use to describe ourselves or others matters, even in subtle ways. In just the same way as information presented first tends to shape the way we interpret all subsequent information (primacy effects), it turns out that **certain words can act as first impression "anchors."**

So, instead of adding up all the traits and information in a description, averaging it out and forming an impression based on that, people tend to use just a few key traits to center their entire impression around. **These traits act like a kind of frame, central axis, or foundation.** See for yourself:

- "Professor Jones is a warm, hardworking, and intelligent expert in his field."
- "Professor Jones is a cold, hardworking, and intelligent expert in his field."

It's easy to see how "hardworking" and "intelligent" can take on negative connotations when in the context of *cold*, but positive ones when in the context of *warm*, right? Lest you think this is merely a primacy effect, try the above sentences with variations on the word order.

It may be that human beings have developed an unconscious shorthand for the way they instantly characterize new people. They need to quickly decide, in essence, *is this person friend or foe?*

There is something very primal and visceral about the warm / cold binary. Our species is warm-blooded and moves about in the daylight, so the very concept of *warmth* signifies life, connection, benevolence, safety, and closeness on an embodied, almost ancient level.

Coldness? That signifies death, separation, and loneliness.

To take advantage of this magical word, **try to find ways to prime people's expectations of you**, so that they are prepared to interpret everything they perceive in you in a kinder, more generous way:

- **Use *warm* in dating profiles.** When describing yourself, use the word warm somewhere, or its variant "warm-hearted." Male or female, you will come across as more likable.
- **Use *warm* in resumes, bios and other professional write-ups.** It's always worth spending time crafting a professional bio

that frames you in the best possible light, but by simple adding the word "warm" you turbo-charge all the traits, accomplishments and abilities you've listed.

- **Use *warm* before giving a performance or presentation.** Wherever possible, find a way to announce a performance or presentation verbally, and sneak in the magic word. For example, ask the person introducing you to say a few carefully crafted sentences. Importantly, you need to make sure that the warm descriptor is applied to *you*, and not just what you're presenting.
- **Where possible, get others to big you up in advance.** In non-professional contexts, recruit friends to put in a good word for you when they can. If you're being set up on a blind date or introduced to a new crowd, get your contact to mention how warm you are.
- ***Think* warm**. Even if you can't find a natural place for the word "warm", you can do a lot to *prime yourself* by thinking in terms of warmth, and letting that attitude radiate out in your body language, gestures, facial expressions, and language choice.
  - You can subliminally convey ideas of likeability by simply making use of metaphors of warmth, words like *bright*, *sunshine,* or *cozy*, smiling, and using open body language.

- o Avoid using verbal and nonverbal expressions that are associated with coldness.
- **Ultimately, remember that warmth = kindness.** If anything, Kelley's study shows us that when it comes to likeability, beneath external markers of intelligence sophistication or status, we are most responsive to markers of human compassion. Always remember that in most social situations, benevolence matters more than perfection, competence, intelligence, or power.

Action step: Do a quick audit of any public descriptors of yourself, whether professional or private. Can you add the magic word anywhere?

Say people's names

Everyday English contains roughly 200,000 words. But when you're talking to someone, there's a single word that is guaranteed to hit their ear a little differently to all the others: their name.

In series of three simple experiments, ("What's in a Name? A Complimentary Means of Persuasion", 1995) Howard, Gengler & Jain found that participants who remembered and used a person's name in conversation increased the chances that the other person would comply with a purchase request.

Think of it this way: on a very basic level, who *knows our name*? Generally, it's the people who already know us and are acquainted with us. Strangers don't.

That means that when you use a person's name, you are sending a very subtle but powerful message:

- I know you
- I'm part of your tribe
- I'm paying attention to *you* specifically

For many people, having someone else remember and use their name feels like a compliment or even a kindness. The fact that Howard, Gengler, & Jain found that people were more willing to buy something from a person who used their name may signal the way names can shift the frame: It's no longer a request from a stranger, but from someone who knows you.

Other studies have found that when people hear their own name, it activates parts of their brains that are connected with attention, identity, and memory (Nakane et.al., 2016; Carmody & Lewsi, 2007; Bao et. al., 2023).

Have you ever suddenly perked up at the mention of your name in conversation? That's a real, measurable effect—**hearing your own name makes you more engaged and perceptive in the conversation.** Your brain thinks, "This concerns me. I'm interested in this."

Want to get people to feel that way about what you're saying? Use their name!

Warning: Don't overdo it. We've all experienced being *over*-named. It can feel weird. Sprinkle the other person's name here and there, but just enough to make them feel remembered and seen.

The Kellogg School of Management showcased another fascinating study ("What's in a Name? Subliminally Activating Trusting Behavior" Huang & Murnighan, 2010) showing that **subliminal exposure to certain names can influence a person's willingness to trust a stranger.**

Yes, subliminal exposure, i.e., seeing a name so quickly that it doesn't register in conscious awareness, can still influence a stranger's perceived trustworthiness.

Here what's they did:

- Participants were asked to make a list of names of people they liked / disliked, and trusted / distrusted.
- While doing an unrelated computer task, the participants were subliminally shown these names. Subliminally = for just 60 milliseconds, i.e., below possible conscious detection.
- Finally, participants were asked to take part in a kind of trust game designed to measure

their degree of willingness to trust a stranger. Participants could decide what proportion of $5 they were willing to give another person. They were told the $5 would be tripled and the recipient given the option of how much they'd return.

The findings:

When people were subliminally shown the liked and trusted names? They sent over an average of around $4. Around half the people sent the full $5 amount.

When people were subliminally shown the disliked and distrusted names? They sent over an average of only $2. Just 15% of people sent over the full $5 amount.

There's more though: The boost in trusting behavior was observed even when only *liked* names were subliminally shown—not names specifically associated with *trustworthiness*. In fact, the only condition that appeared to lower trust was exposure to names that were both disliked and distrusted.

Let's zoom out. Obviously, we don't have the means to subliminally influence people in the way these researchers did. But there are some interesting insights for us nevertheless:

- **Subconscious associations do matter.** When people are exposed to names that they associate with trustworthiness and

likeability, they tend to respond—even if they're not aware what's happening.
- **If names affect us subconsciously, they can affect us consciously, too.** This gives "name dropping" a whole new meaning. In casual conversation, mention names of people that are associated with the kind of positive feelings and ideas you'd like to bring to that relationship. This will activate certain psychological schemas and gently influence the tone of the conversation.
- **You can create trustworthiness by association.** Mentioning the name of someone with positive associations activates the listener's *relational schema*—which is the internal network of people you know and trust. When you say a trustworthy person's name, the effect is very subtly akin to them vouching for you.

Action step: Make it a goal to mention at least two names in your next conversation: the name of the other person, and the name of someone you have good reason to believe they both like and trust. This simple habit will make you feel more likeable and more trustworthy.

Politeness is (usually) the default

Christian Danescu-Niculescu-Mizil is an associate professor in the department of informational science at Cornell University. He is interested in the way that computing and human conversation overlap, and together with a research team, he investigated how politeness works in online conversations—including those using AI (Danescu-Niculescu-Mizil et al. 2013, "Computational Approaches to Politeness").

Using machine learning, the team analyzed online message data sets and tried to hunt out linguistic patterns that correlated with politeness.

The paper, published in the journal *Computation and Language*, presented some interesting ideas:

- Politeness can actually be perceived by computers.
- Politeness varies somewhat according to context—for example people making requests tend to be noticeably more polite than normal.
- Politeness appears to be correlated with power—the more power, the less politeness!

So far, none of this may seem very surprising.

While the authors are interested in politeness in order to build better software (i.e., "computational politeness") we can apply some of their findings to our own social lives.

Signs of politeness are almost universal:

- Say please and thank you

- Be less blunt and direct, and soften a statement by turning it into a question; for example, "That's wrong" is softer when expressed as, "I wonder if this might be wrong?"
- Use hedging phrases to make your statements less forceful; for example, instead of "This won't work" say, "I think this maybe won't work."
- Use phrases like "I would appreciate it if…" and "Would it be possible…"
- Politeness is also expressed nonverbally—smile, use open and warm body language, and avoid interrupting people.

On the other hand, the study does show us the other side of politeness: It can sometimes work against us to be too polite!

Why? Because **those who are slightly more forceful and direct may in some contexts be perceived as more powerful.**

Let's tread carefully.

Politeness, willingness to cooperate, courtesy, respect, and being accommodating are all broadly associated with the psychological trait of *agreeableness*—which is strongly correlated with good social outcomes.

BUT there are occasionally times when this sort of agreeableness may be perceived as submission or weakness.

Though blatant incivility and bad manners are *never* a good look, you may need to be blunter and more direct when:

- You're asserting a boundary
- You're protecting or defending yourself
- You're trying to clarify a mistake or misunderstanding

Occasionally, there may be a trade-off between being perceived as likeable and being perceived as powerful. Choose wisely.

Action step: Take stock of your own politeness levels in your current relationships. Is there someone you could stand to show a little more courtesy? Is there someone who you need to be firmer and more direct towards?

The gain-loss theory of attraction

OK, question time. Take a look at each of the following four people and their attitudes towards you. Can you rank in order which person *you* like the most?

- **Person 1:** They don't like you. But then again, they never did.
- **Person 2:** They liked you at first, but as time goes on they seem to like you less and less.
- **Person 3:** They weren't sure about you at first, but somehow every time you meet, they seem to like you a little more.
- **Person 4:** They liked you from the moment they first met you, and they still like you.

It's clear that Person 3 and person 4 are likeable since they like you... but is there a difference between them?

According to one research study, *yes*.

Aronson & Linder's classic 1965 research demonstrated that **we are influenced not just by other peoples' opinions about us, but how those opinions change over time.**

Perhaps counterintuitively, most of us are **more drawn to people whose feelings towards us slowly improve over time**, than to those who have consistently held a positive opinion about us.

In other words, strangely, we find those who are "slow to warm" more likeable overall than those who easily and readily like us and never change their opinion.

How can we explain this?

Aronson & Linder gave an explanation that relied on the concept of *reinforcement*—when someone's opinion of us improves, we might feel like we've done something to earn it, and their approval feels like a reward. This reinforces our liking for them and confirms their approval as something of real value—that is, not just given away to anyone as a default!

The "Gain-loss theory of attraction" explains it like this:

- When we start with nothing (i.e., people are cool or neutral towards us) and then gradually their liking for us grows, this **feels like a gain**.
  - The researchers claim that this condition is preferred, even above having someone's consistent liking.
- When we start with something (i.e., people like us immediately) and then the other person gradually withdraws that liking, this **feels like a loss.**
- Compare this with a person who likes us but always did, or doesn't like us but never did—both of these things **feel like neither a loss nor gain.**

To put it all together:

Gain > Consistently Positive > Consistently Negative > Loss

We like the person who warms to us gradually over time more than we like the person who has always liked us. And we may dislike the person who starts disliking us over time more than we dislike the person who we never clicked with anyway.

A shift from disapproval to approval is more psychologically rewarding than consistent approval, and the reverse shift is more painful than plain dislike.

Let's think carefully about how we apply these findings to our own lives:

Change matters more than consistency. This implies a few interesting things.

- You don't need to rush or force an instant liking with new people. You don't have to over-adapt. A slow burn takes time and patience, but will ultimately feel more satisfying. Let your warmth slowly reveal itself.
- You don't have to make a big impact right out of the gate. In fact, being too ready to show your own liking early on can paradoxically cheapen that liking in the eyes of the other person, and weaken that sense of reward or reinforcement
- You don't have to work too hard to flatter people early on, especially if you're not being genuine. Relax and don't sweat minor disagreements or points of misalignment. You don't have to frontload all your charm or deliberately downplay the rougher edges of your personality!

In fairy tales and old school romances, the princess is always slightly hesitant to be rescued by the brave knight, but comes around eventually. Though politically incorrect and perfectly cheesy, this dynamic reveals an important truth about human interactions and the way we value one another's liking and approval: **people like to think that they have won you over.**

Have you ever really enjoyed someone's company only to realize that they are that warm and friendly to *everyone*? The reason it stings is that another person's liking—even if superficial—feels like a validation of us a people.

> → A warning to the people-pleasers among us: if you are too "nice" to everyone without distinction, this sense of validation disappears. Ironically, the other person may feel *less* seen and *less* valued.

Now, a caveat—in a distorted form, this theory explains why things like "negging" or backhanded handed compliments can sometimes work. The idea is to deliberately insult someone so that when you do show them liking, they'll be more receptive to your advances (i.e., it will be perceived as a gain, and the insulter perceived as more likeable).

Using the gain-loss theory ethically means never deliberately giving a false impression of not liking someone. Treating people poorly or making veiled insults is not just immoral, it's more likely to land you in the "Person 1" category.

Action step: When first getting to know someone, relax, and be neutral. Adjust your mindset: You're not attending a make-or-break interview. You're just laying a solid foundation for something to develop in future, over time. The next time you meet that person, warm things up a notch. Go slow.

Chapter 6: It's how you frame things

The art of "self-handicapping"

Imagine one day you're at the circus and watching a strongman give a performance. You know the kind of thing: lugging tree trunks, flipping giant tires and lifting spheres of solid concrete.

Now imagine the strongman as he approaches a barbell laden with a record-breaking amount of weight.

He huffs and puffs, claps chalk on his hands, huff and puffs again.

He squares up and tries to lift it but stops, hesitates, and steps back again. The crowd watches, rapt. It looks almost impossible.

Then he approaches again, he tries—he fails! The crowd erupts in concerned mutters.

He tries again, and fails a second time. By now the crowd is really doubtful.

But when he tries for the third time, neck veins bulging and face red, *he lifts the bar*, and to wild cheers from the crowd.

Later you learn that all these failed attempts were actually deliberate and perfectly staged. As a performer, the strongman understood that the crowd always finds it far more entertaining and psychologically satisfying to first draw attention to certain obstacles and difficulties before overcoming them. Pick that bar up too easily? Well, there's no fun in that!

The term **"self-handicapping"** describes this kind of dynamic. **It refers to creating or drawing attention to barriers before successfully accomplishing a performance task** (Jones & Berglas, 1978; Jones & Wortman, 1973). And it instantly creates a feeling of liking, respect, and admiration.

In essence, you point to a handicap or (in the case of the circus strongman) you exaggerate or even create that handicap.

If you fail? You can save face by pointing to the handicap.

But if you succeed? Then that success will be seen as *particularly* impressive, given the obstacle.

It's a win-win.

Self-handicapping was originally studied as a naturally occurring defense mechanism, i.e., where people try to protect their self-image and maintain a degree of control during high-stakes performances.

For our purposes, however, we can consciously use self-handicapping to come across as more likeable, humble, and trustworthy. How?

- **Mention (small) obstacles before a performance.** It can be quite charming and relatable, for instance, to note your own nervousness before giving a recital, or to give a little caveat about how you haven't done as much preparation as you'd hoped before a speech.
- **Be strategically humble.** It's not enough to self-handicap—you need to follow through! The effect works if you then do deliver a competent performance. A little vulnerability makes it easier for your audience to root for you, and celebrate more when you do succeed.
- **Don't be cocky.** The reverse effect is to perform with unshakeable confidence, even arrogance, and have people less impressed even though your delivery is flawless. Remember the circus strongman, and allow people to see just how hard it is to lift that metaphorical bar. Let them see you struggle *a little*, and they'll be all the more impressed when you overcome it.

Self-handicapping is best when you feel fairly confident in your own abilities, and when you'd like to show off a little but *without* incurring the social penalty of appearing to brag. People who are perceived as both talented yet humble and down-to-earth are extremely likeable.

Warning: Avoid downplaying your performance *after* you've successfully concluded it. Under promise, over deliver, gracefully accept any praise, and then move on. Being self-deprecating can actually backfire. You may either be seen to have low self-esteem, be "fishing for compliments", or both. Saying "Oh it was nothing," when it clearly was, risks coming across as insincere. Just say thank you.

Action step: It may feel a little phony, but take the time to pre-prepare some things you can say both before and after a performance. This will help you frame yourself in the best possible way and will help relieve any nervousness or self-consciousness.

Humor is your secret weapon

It's not exactly breaking news that funny people are likeable people.

What's less commonly known is that there are many, many different *types* of humor, and not all of them are associated with social success. When it comes to humor, it's not what you do, but the way that you do it. Let's take a closer look.

Humor can be tricky to put your finger on... but that doesn't mean that social scientists and psychologist haven't made the attempt! What is currently known about the way humor influences our social mastery?

Your humor style influences how other people perceive your personality and overall likeability (Kuiper & Leite, 2009):

Affiliative and **self-enhancing humor** styles are said to be associated with positive personality traits and are perceived as more likeable socially.

- **Affiliative humor =** Benevolent, self-accepting, and focused on building up relationships. This kind of humor eases group tensions, amuses people, puts everyone at ease and makes people feel happy and relaxed. There is no "butt of the joke."
- **Self-enhancing humor =** Being good natured and able to laugh at yourself or look at the funny side of life's difficulties. This kind of humor is really coping and healthy self-regulation in disguise.

On the other hand, **aggressive** or **self-defeating humor** styles are generally associated with maladaptive personality traits and are less favored socially.

- **Aggressive humor** = Humor at someone's expense. This is targeted humor that harms, such as sarcasm, teasing, mockery, and anything that disregards or belittles another person under the guise of playfulness.
- **Self-defeating humor =** This is harmful humor directed at the self, usually as an attempt to gain others' approval or sympathy. Unsurprisingly, self-deprecating humor can be perceived as low self-esteem or passive aggression and is *not* socially appealing.

We all have a slightly different style of humor, but it's worth paying attention to the overall *tone and quality*, as well as the *direction or target* of our humor.

To effectively use humor in social situations, make jokes that point out the amusing idiosyncrasies of life or circumstances, without making yourself or other people pay the price.

Affiliative and self-enhancing humor types have been consistently associated with higher emotional intelligence, greater social competence, robust mental health (Yip & Martin, 2006)… and even your attractiveness as a mate (Bressler & Balshine, 2006).

Is self-deprecating humor really so bad?

Poking fun at yourself *can* endear you to others socially and make you appear more likeable, trustworthy, and relatable... but there are nuances.

A study by Greengross and Miller (2008) suggests that people find self-deprecating humor attractive, but only when used by "high status individuals."

If you're a low status individual? Self-depreciation just doesn't seem as appealing.

The takeaway: Self-deprecating humor seems to work because of the surprising and amusing *contrast* between what is said and the observable reality. When high-status individuals say something that downplays that status, it's funny and unexpected.

Example: Someone wins an Olympic gold medal and jokes on the podium, "What do you think, should I grow my chest hair out and wear this to the club?" They seem charming and likeable.

However, if you suspect you're closer to an, ahem, *low status individual*, your best chance at humor might be to go the other way.

Example: You crash your car during your driver's test and turn to the instructor saying, "You know, I think I'm getting the hang of this." It works because of the *contrast* between what is said and the obvious reality. It's funny, but it also makes you likeable because you seem self-aware and resilient.

If you must use self-deprecating humor, here are a few rules to play by:

Use self-defeating humor to defuse. If you've made a mistake or been called out, be ready and willing to laugh at yourself. Likewise, plenty of potential conflicts and frictions can be avoided if you use a little self-deprecating humor when someone *else* has messed up and apologized. This way you will come across as forgiving, gracious, and highly likeable. You smooth tensions *and* boost your perceived status.

Use self-defeating humor to boost morale. Self-deprecating humor can be a powerful response to failure or adversity, especially if you are in a leadership position Gkorezis & Bellou, 2016). Humble optimism signals trustworthiness and the ability to dust yourself off and keep going.

Use a light touch. Poke *a little* fun at yourself—but don't go overboard. Keep it gentle, maintain a degree of genuine self-respect and self-acceptance, and mix it up with other humor types.

Warning: Unfortunately, in an attempt to be perceived as witty or clever, people can resort to humor that is too controversial, try-hard, or confusing—this creates a poor impression and risks being misunderstood. Things to steer clear of:

- Sarcasm
- "Deadpan" humor
- Being edgy, offensive, or controversial
- "Roasting", put-downs, or insults
- Political humor
- Putting yourself down
- "Off color" humor—vulgarity, swearing, coarseness

Generally, these are all fairly high-risk approaches that don't create real connection and chemistry anyway—especially with people you don't know that well.

Beware of making your humor too complicated. If a joke relies on complex word play and obscure references, your audience may feel more confused than amused; the extra time it takes for them to figure out what you mean only puts up an additional barrier to connection, and may make those who don't "get it" feel left out.

Jokes should be *easy to digest*. This kind of humor might not feel very slick and sophisticated, but it's about mutual good feelings, rather than ego and performance. As a rule, it's usually better to *be obvious rather than subtle*—i.e., don't leave people genuinely wondering whether you're joking or not, as this instantly dampens rapport.

Finally, *know your audience*. Long-time friends you've known intimately for decades? You can probably play free and loose because you understand their humor. Complete strangers you've just met? For their sake and yours, play it safe!

Focus on friendly vibes, fun, warmth, making people feel good, and jokes that demonstrate a kind of stubborn optimism and genuine playfulness. You don't need to crack wise or be super entertaining!

Action step: Spend a little time thinking of the perfect joke or funny anecdote that you can use in any social situation. Without rehearsing it word for word, get comfortable telling this joke or anecdote ahead of time. You'll have an easy way to build good vibes without having to think of something on the spot.

Don't be afraid to ask for help

Here's a mental exercise: Think for a moment about an acquaintance in your social group, i.e., someone you like and know, but who you wouldn't quite call a good friend. Now imagine that you're in a pinch and need help.

How comfortable do you feel asking this person to assist you, and do you a much-needed favor?

The second part of the mental exercise goes like this: Imagine that this same acquaintance gets in touch and asks the very same favor of *you*.

How willing are you to help them out?

If you find that the answer to the first question and the second question don't quite line up, then you're not alone. It's exactly what a study published in the *Journal of Personality and Social Psychology* found (Flynn & Lake, 2008):

People tend to *greatly underestimate* the willingness of others to comply with a request for help.

Multiples surveyed studies show that this is a stable bias, and that the mismatch can be as much as 50%.

Why do we tend to imagine that others will be less generous than we are?

Why are we reluctant to express a need for help?

Flynn and Lake's explanation: In their study, people seeking help tended to focus on how much it would "cost" for the other person to comply with the request, but they didn't focus on the cost of *not* complying (social pressure, guilt, etc.).

The takeaways:

- Need help? You may worry about offending or inconveniencing people, but bear in mind that you're probably underestimating the other person's willingness to help. Just ask!

We might add to Flynn and Lake's analysis that we underestimate how much people actually *enjoy* giving.

For the same reason that many of us are uncomfortable with the vulnerability of asking, we may be more comfortable with feeling needed, and playing the role of someone who can generously help.

And this leads us to a deeper insight not relationships more generally: that we tend to have mistaken intuitions around giving, receiving, and "social debt." Let's take a closer look.

The Ben Franklin effect

Contrary to expectations, **people actually tend to like you more after doing a favor for you—** and not the other way around. This fascinating psychological phenomenon has been called the Ben Franklin Effect.

The classic 1969 experiment by Jecker & Landy described how study participants did a Q&A competition for which they received monetary rewards.

- Then, the participants were broken into three groups:
    - **Group A**: The researcher personally asked them to give back the money they'd won, explaining that he personally needed the money.
    - **Group B**: The same request was made but by a secretary, who explained that departmental funds were lacking.

- **Group C**: No request was made. The participants kept their winnings.

The results were surprising. When interviewed about their degree of liking for the researcher, it was participants in Group 1 that showed the most fondness, indicating that the favor of returning money didn't weaken their opinion of the researcher, but actually bolstered it.

How can we explain this?

Cognitive dissonance = the mental discomfort that arises when our actions don't quite line up with our inner attitudes and beliefs.

In this case, it goes like this: If you help someone, then it would feel quite strange to simultaneously hold a negative opinion of that person. You resolve this tension or dissonance by adjusting your feelings to match your actions—i.e., you conclude that you *do* like them after all (otherwise why would you have done them the favor?).

Subsequent studies (for example Niiya, 2015) have found this bias quite robust, even across different contexts and cultures.

The Ben Franklin Effect is so named because its first written description appears in the famous man's autobiography. He explains how a rival legislator was converted into a good friend not by Franklin doing favors for him, but precisely the reverse:

> *"Having heard that he had in his library a certain very scarce and curious book, I wrote a note to him, expressing my desire of perusing that book, and requesting he would do me the favour of lending it to me for a few days. He sent it immediately, and I return'd it in about a week with another note, expressing strongly my sense of the favour. When we next met in the House, he spoke to me (which he had never done before), and with great civility; and he ever after manifested a readiness to serve me on all occasions, so that we became great friends, and our friendship continued to his death."*

The effect is counterintuitive, but real. Not only are people more willing to help than we guess, but asking for their help may actually make them like us even more.

A few tips:

- **The way you ask matters.** Frame the request clearly as *a favor from them to you.* Allow other people to feel that they possess the means to make your life easier.
- **Don't be in too big a hurry to return the favor.** Reciprocity does matter, but being too quick to return the favor can sometimes be perceived as neutralizing the goodwill they've already generated. A little "friendly debt" joins people together more strongly

than perfect egalitarianism (more on this in a later chapter).

- **Keep it small, but genuine.** Obviously at some point, a favor really is too big to ask of anyone. Since the effect appears regardless of the size of the favor, ask for help with a small but genuine need.

Individualism and self-sufficiency are valorized in the modern world, particularly in some cultures. However, for human beings, deep social bonds have always flourished in the context of mutual *need*.

When you give other people the opportunity to help you in your need, you make them feel like they matter, like they're important, and like your wellbeing is dependent in some small way on their generosity.

Be willing to ask people for help, even if it feels a little scary, awkward, or uncomfortable. That feeling of vulnerability is precisely the mechanism through which others can connect with you more deeply.

Action step: Today, think of an acquaintance or almost-friend that you'd like to get closer to. Think of a small favor you can ask them. If that doesn't feel natural, consider just asking their advice or opinion on something, or see if they can help you solve a minor problem. You may be surprised at their readiness to help!

The bystander effect

In 1964, the murder of Kitty Genovese shocked the world, not just because of the senselessness of the act, but because it occurred in broad daylight, where several witnesses looked on—and utterly failed to intervene.

The public wanted to know how it was possible that people could stand by as someone was murdered before their very eyes. The social scientists wanted to know, too (Latane & Darley, 1970) and today their findings have shaped what we understand about helping behavior, and in particular what's called the bystander effect.

In short, the **bystander effect is the phenomenon whereby people are less likely to help a person in need when others are present.**

To explore the effect in a clinical setting, Latane and Darley put study participants in a situation where a confederate pretended to suddenly have a seizure. How would people respond? Did they help?

The answer is yes—when people believed that they were the only ones who could help, then a full **85%** took steps to intervene.

However, when participants believed that other people were also present, just **31%** of them took helping action.

Why the discrepancy?

In emergency situations, Latane and Darley explain, there is a kind of "diffusion of responsibility" which is essentially the assumption, "There are a lot of people here; somebody else will help." Of course, if *everyone* feels this way, then nobody will help. In fact, the more people there are, the more pronounced the effect.

While the Kitty Genovese case made people say, "There were so many people, how is it that none of them helped?" we now know that it's precisely because there were so many people that none of them helped!

The bystander effect is a robust and predictable quirk of human behavior, but Latane and Darley explain that it's possible to consciously override it:

- Step 1: Notice what is happening
- Step 2: Interpret it as an emergency
- Step 3: Take responsibility
- Step 4: Know how to help
- Step 5: Make the decision to help

If a person fails at any of these steps, they are unlikely to help. They may not be aware of the problem, they may not accurately perceive what's happening, they may not feel responsible, and even if they do feel responsible, they may not know how to help. Finally, they may simply choose not to—recall than in both the study's test conditions, there were always some people who simply didn't.

Latane and Darley's research laid the foundation for understanding emergency response behavior and has had a lasting impact on social psychology. But we can also draw our own insights from this research classic:

- In social settings, assume that your default is *not* to take responsibility—and be alert and ready to correct this bias.
- In a group, most people will default to no-action. That means that if you are the one to take initiative and help, you'll stand out as more trustworthy and dependable.
- Don't underestimate either your power or your responsibility in a social situation. Statistically, it's not always true that "somebody else will do it." Instead, *be that somebody* and go first. This is a capacity demonstrated by leaders.

The bystander effect shines an unflattering light on human nature. Most of us possess a kind of innate laziness; if we believe there's a chance somebody else might step up, then we're perfectly happy to forego doing something useful, kind, or necessary.

In Latane and Darley's studies, just *one third* of people chose to actively help when others were present—the rest shirked the responsibility.

Let's be honest: Most people are out for themselves only, and even though they might claim to be friends when times are good, in an emergency they are reluctant to actually *do* anything for others.

If, however, you can understand this, then you can:

- Be aware that not everyone who claims to be a friend will necessarily help you when the chips are down.
- Consciously choose to be a part of the 31% yourself.
- Set yourself apart as someone who is engaged, reliable, alert and present.

Deep down, we all want good, trustworthy people in our "tribes." Life can be tough and people are reluctant to invest emotionally in people who will run away when things get difficult.

Make efforts to let others observe your willingness to help, and your responsiveness to their distress—even if it's only in tiny ways.

This is about more than being polite or doing favors. Rather, it's about taking initiative to help.

Action step: Of course, real emergencies are rare and unpredictable. But prick your ears and pay close attention when someone is struggling, feeling bullied, lost, confused, or dealing with something unexpected. Be ready to step up and help *immediately*. If you realize that someone is upset, don't assume that they already have a vast and supportive network around them. *You* may actually be their best bet!

Step in. You'll be seen as warmer and more likeable, but even better, people will feel like they can *trust* you, and that trust is the foundation on which you can build real relationships.

Cheat code: The door-in-the-face technique

Cialdini et al. (1975) formally studied a "compliance strategy" that old school door-to-door salesmen have known about for a long time. In a paper title "Reciprocal Concessions Procedure for Inducing Compliance: The Door-in-the-Face Technique" the authors explored a way that people can game certain unspoken rules about *reciprocity*.

Take a look at their research design:

- First, study participants were broken into two groups.
- Group 1 was confronted with a pretty big ask. In this case, it was a request for them to volunteer as a counsellor for juvenile delinquents (hey, it was the 70s—this terminology was considered standard!), for two hours a week, for two years.
- Unsurprisingly, most people said no.

- Immediately afterwards, the participants were presented with a smaller request: would they mind doing a mere two-hour zoo trip with those same ~~juvenile delinquents~~ adolescents with legal system involvement?
- Group 2 was also presented with the zoo request, but without having heard the big request first.

Let's look at the results:

People in Group 2 were far less likely to agree to the small request than people in group 1. In fact, the difference was significant: compliance in Group 1 was around 50%, whereas in Group 2 it was only around 17%. That means that compliance in Group 1 was *almost triple* that of Group 2.

In short, **people are more likely to comply with a small request if it follows a big request**.

How can we explain the result?

The idea is that people feel a sense of reciprocity—especially in more clearly transactional relationships. The exchange goes like this:

- A person makes a large and unreasonable request.
- The other person refuses.

- The first person moderates that request, and this concession is perceived as a mild compromise… even a subtle favor.
- For this subtle favor, the other person feels a slight pressure to acquiesce ("He's backed down a little, I guess I can too").
- The person agrees to the second request.

Of course, **the door-in-the-face technique is a way of deliberately exploiting this social quirk**. The asker's real goal all along is actually the second request—they just use the first request to:

- Make the second one seem small by comparison.
- Establish an illusory state of reciprocity.

In the sales context, this technique is rightly seen as unscrupulous and is often recognized for what it is. However, we can certainly use the *principle* more benignly in our own social lives. Here's how:

Be mindful of the way you *frame* and *sequence* things. We've seen that it's important to take care of how you present yourself. Likewise, it's important to take care of how you present information and requests.

Want people to do something for you?

- **Don't under-ask**—in fact, ask for more than you hope to get. That way, any outcome is good. Either they'll say yes, or they'll agree but to less—which you were always going to be happy with. On the other hand, if a person complies to a request that you then add to, you risk causing resentment.

- **Use guilt and obligation very sparingly.** You *may* get people to do what you want by exploiting their sense of reciprocity, but they certainly won't like it, and you may not be able to repeat the trick. Recall that compliance in Group 1 was still only 50% - which means that the other 50% refused—and probably still felt a little put out.
- **Frame compliance as their generosity—not your entitlement.** The idea is that complying with something small is a bonus over a flat-out no. You need to try and frame their compliance as a sign of their unnecessary and additional generosity—i.e., you are not disappointed they said no to the big thing, but thrilled they said yes to the small thing.

What do you do if people still refuse the second smaller request? Drop it. Even when people fail to comply with your request, the best way forward is to act like this is a perfectly reasonable reaction from them. Thank them for giving you *something*, even if it's just their time or consideration.

Be graceful, be polite, and don't push it.

Remember self-fulfilling social stereotypes—if you treat people like they're kind, generous, and reasonable, they're more likely to act that way. Consider the long game: if you graciously accept their refusal *this* time, the rules of reciprocity might make them more willing to acquiesce *next time*.

Action step: Take the door-in-the-face technique out for a test drive and see it in action for yourself. Is there a favor you need from someone? Resist the urge to downplay your request and see what happens when you push it in the other direction!

Chapter 7: Common misconceptions

Socialize—even if you don't always feel like it!

Misconception 1: *Socializing is kind of optional. You don't have to do it unless you feel like it.*

Loneliness has serious consequences for mental *and* physical health. A study published in the journal Neuron Delgado, Fareri & Chang (2023) that social connection is not just about recreation or relaxation—it's actually a powerful way for individuals and groups to self-regulate.

Social connection creates but also sustains itself. Socializing is its own cause and effect. This means:

- The more you socialize, the easier you find it, and the more you want to do it.
- On the other hand, the *less* you socialize, the more difficult you may find it, and the harder it will feel to get back into it again.

When you socialize, those happy, connected feelings are actually a **sensation of reward**—

and this acts as a significant protectant against stress and isolation.

Social isolation interferes with your brain's stress response mechanisms.

Social connection buffers and supports your resilience against that stress.

When you experience positive social interactions, your brain's reward circuitry is activated and you feel motivated to do more. **So while we might think that we need to feel good in order to socialize, the opposite is true: We will feel good because we socialize.**

But that's not all—socializing literally helps you think with others, as you align perspectives and establish a shared reality that makes sense to you both—again, very satisfying!

When things are ticking over as they should, these things create a kind of positive feedback loop.

- You socialize
- Your brain feels good, and rewards you
- That sense of reward motivates you to connect further
- You socialize again

Think of it this way: **Socializing is a kind of collective immune system.** Through others, you access a kind of relational stability, and stress regulation that keeps you feeling strong, balanced, and at ease.

Sounds great. But there's a catch—the feedback loop can also go the other way:

- You avoid socializing
- You feel isolated and disconnected
- You lack motivation to seek people out
- You continue to avoid socializing…

Negative loops can also be established when we experience negative social interactions. A few awkward or painful encounters and we may decide that people are too much trouble, and that we prefer our own company anyway.

But there's a cost: We lose that stress-regulation ability, and we lose a sense of alignment and empathy with others. This makes people feel even harder to understand or care about and, since breaking that ice just keeps getting harder, we may grow more and more avoidant.

We lose shared perspective.

We lose that sense of belonging to a shared reality.

It may even start to feel like we live in a completely different universe from everyone else…

The way out? **Socialize—*even if you don't always feel like it.***

In fact, you could almost say that wanting to avoid other people is an early warning sign that you need to seek them out!

Do you have to hang out with people who are bad for you? Of course not. Often, you may not want to enter into a social group's "shared reality" or align yourself with their feelings, thoughts, and perspectives. Why not?

Well, social connection *can* be:

- Exhausting
- Time consuming
- Exposing
- Risky
- Boring
- Difficult
- Annoying

… but that doesn't mean it's not worth it! The sooner we can convince ourselves that (healthy) social connections are non-negotiable, the sooner we'll take our social life as seriously as other health habits like exercise and nutrition.

Action step: Turn a vicious cycle into a "virtuous cycle." The next time you're feeling anti-social and avoidant, force yourself to reach out, even if just in a small way.

Share your thoughts.

Step into someone else's world for a little while.

It doesn't have to be deep and meaningful, either!

Afterwards, check in with yourself—most of the time, you'll feel glad that you made the effort. The next time you feel avoidant, remind yourself of successful past social interactions, and how pushing past that initial resistance ultimately brought rewards.

Misery loves (similar) company

Misconception 2: *Being a good friend means doing whatever you can to cheer people up when they're struggling. We need to "be there" for our friends when they're having a hard time.*

A paper published in the Journal *The Psychology of Affiliation,* Stanley Schachter (1959) devised a study that went as follows:

- Study participants were informed that as part of the research, they would be receiving electric shocks. The researchers never intended to give the shocks, but by saying they would, they induced a state of anxiety.
- Some of the participants were told that the shocks they'd receive would be quite painful, while others were told the shocks would be mild.
- After being told about the shocks, the participants were then asked whether they wanted to sit in a waiting room:
    - Alone
    - Or with other people

- In other test conditions, some were given the option of sitting with people who were:
  - In the same situation, i.e., also anxious
  - Or nor in the same situation, i.e., not anxious like them
- The researchers carefully recorded whether the participants wanted to be anxious on their own or with others, and if the latter, what kind of company they most desired.

Before you read on to see what the results were, ask yourself how *you* would feel in this situation.

If you're feeling anxious, who do you most feel like being around?

Schachter and his associates found that:

- **When anxiety was high** (painful shocks were anticipated) participants wanted to wait with other people—but *only if those people were also anxious*, like them.
- **When anxiety was lower** (only mild shocks were anticipated) participants weren't that interested in waiting with other people.

Interestingly, one thing was clear: When people felt anxious, they did *not* want to be around people who were not.

So, this means that the old saying, "misery loves company" is partly true. We might automatically assume that people want and need company when they're feeling scared, overwhelmed, or stressed, but that's not always true, and the *kind* of company matters!

Why should people prefer to be in the company of those who are in similar emotional states to them?

- **Perhaps shared experience holds more value than abstract empathy.** Anyone can *say*, "I feel you" but if someone is literally in the same position as you, you already know that they understand how you feel... because they're feeling it too.
- **Perhaps other people's positive emotions heighten awareness of our own negative emotions.** It's a question of contrast and comparison. When we're with people on the same emotional frequency as us, there is a sense of affiliation and bonding. When we see them in a completely different state of mind, we may feel even more isolated and less accepting of our condition.
- **Perhaps other people's positive emotions serve to invalidate our negative ones.** If someone else feels as we do, it subtly authenticates our appraisal of the situation and makes us feel like our response makes sense. On the other hand, it's easy to feel embarrassed, angry, or confused by our emotion if we appear to be the only ones who have it!

Schachter's research tells us something interesting about how people can comfort one another in their distress. Certain conventions around what empathy actually looks like may not be grounded in reality.

How can we apply all this practically to our own social lives?

- People experiencing **mild or moderate stress** might benefit most from simply being left alone. We need to be honest if our need to help (or our need to give the impression of helpfulness!) is actually providing real comfort. If someone appears annoyed, overwhelmed, or stressed:
    - **Offer to help, but just once.** Repeated unwanted offers of help can actually start to feel like demands. Let people know you're there for them, but be willing to respect their need for alone time.
    - **Be useful.** Support, comfort, and reassurance don't always look like an earnest therapy session or a big serious "talk." Sometimes, it's enough to simply notice that someone is struggling, and to proactively take steps to lighten their burden or make their lives easier. Is your partner flustered with the clutter in the living room? Quietly take a moment to tidy some of it up.

- If someone is experiencing **high anxiety and stress**, they may well want company, but not just any old company.
    - **Hold the "toxic positivity."** Avoid offering advice, platitudes, or suggestions to "cheer up." This is likely to make you seem insensitive and make them feel even worse.
    - **Match and mirror.** How are they feeling? Find subtle ways to reflect that feeling back to them—this is a form of empathy that may feel particularly satisfying in distressing moments. Of course, you don't have to be down in the pit with them, but harmonize your emotional tone with theirs. Pay attention to their voice, body language, and facial expression—and reflect the same back to them.
    - **Self-disclose—a little.** Chances are you won't be in the exact situation as they are. But you may have experienced something similar in the past. You can mention this experience, but carefully—the idea is never to one-up their distress or frame yourself as an expert. Instead of "I'm so great I already figured out this thing that has you stumped" the vibe should be, "you're not alone."

Action step: Finally, there is one more way to apply Schachter's results: When strengthening new friendships and connections, it's worth finding ways to **do hard things together.**

That may be skydiving, challenging sports, a grueling hike, a difficult jigsaw puzzle, or even the ordeal of navigating the car park at a giant festival. What matters is the opportunity to sync emotionally.

If you can commiserate and survive an uncomfortable or challenging experience together, you can quickly drum up those feelings of affiliation, trust, and connection. After all, how many times have you heard people say things like, "This is my good friend. We've been through so much together"?

There's power in shared adversity.

The advice paradox

Misconception 3: *As the German proverb says, "Never give advice unless asked. The wise won't need it, the fool won't heed it."*

Question: Why do people ask for advice?

This seems like a no-brainer, right? They ask for advice because they want advice. They want help and guidance on how to solve a predicament they're in.

Or do they?

Another question: Why do people *give* advice?

Is it really just because they want to be helpful and useful?

This fascinating area of advice and decision-making has been investigated by Brooks and colleagues (2014), who coined the term **advice paradox.**

The paradox is this: people often seek advice, but then don't always take it—even if the advice is pretty good.

Brooks et. al. explain that when people ask for advice, there are actually *two* competing tensions inside them:

1. They want help
2. ...but they also want to feel competent, independent, and capable

Basically, **it's an ego thing.**

When a person is experiencing a problem or facing the limits of their ability or understanding, it can put a big dent in their self-image. It implies a lack or limitation and suggests that they can't succeed without outside intervention.

Now, needing help and advice doesn't imply all this, but it may sometimes *feel* like it!

Let's look at things from the advice-givers perspective. Why do they give advice? There are also reasons here:

1. They want to help
2. ...but they also want to feel respected, powerful, valued, needed, and important

Again, that second point comes down to ego.

Some people ask for advice and don't take it (ego).

Some people offer advice when it's not requested (ego).

So, how can we apply all of this?

So, the German proverb is not entirely correct. There is nothing innately wrong with giving or requesting advice... but we need to be mindful of *how* we do it.

The golden advice rule is that it should always feel *collaborative*.

When giving advice:

- **Wait till you're asked**. It may sometimes feel wildly tempting to make an obvious suggestion, but remind yourself that unless people actually ask, what they most need is just for you to listen and be present.
- **Don't undermine their agency**. Frame advice as a question, a suggestion, or an invitation for them to collaborate on problem-solving.
  - Instead of: "You should..."
  - Try "What do you think would happen if you...?"

- **Be mindful.** Try to be honest about your motivations; do you genuinely want to help, or are you just enjoying playing the role of the person who has all the answers?
- **Don't take things personally.** Be careful if the other person is feeling embarrassed, defensive, or insecure—they are simply not in the position to take advice, no matter how well-meaning. Don't be too worried if people don't take your advice—the value for them might have simply been in the fact that you cared enough to give it.
- **Recognize the paradox.** Realize that if a person has asked for advice, they have deliberately made themselves a little vulnerable. Respect this vulnerability by *not* adopting an attitude of superiority. You'll win their trust big time. The vibe you want to convey is: "Oh, you already know the answer to this, you've just temporarily forgotten, and I'm reminding you."

When asking for advice or receiving it:

- **Actually ask!** Sometimes, you can ask for advice just because you want to include, flatter, or show respect to the other person. It communicates: "I value your perspective; I respect you and I trust you enough to include you in my decision-making process."
- **Don't take offense.** If someone gives you unsolicited advice or makes you feel inferior, take a step back and realize that this likely

says more about them than it does you and your situation. In fact, the advice people give you provides precious insight into the way they think:
- What kind of suggestions and solutions do they offer? Look closely and these will tell you what they value and how they see the world.
- What aspect of your situation are they responding to most? This can tell you what they see in you—which tells you a lot about their own struggles, history and perspective.
- Is someone deliberately trying to advise, support or guide you? Though clumsy, this may be a clear message that they care and are trying to connect. Take it as a signal that they want to be closer.

- **Say thank you.** Even if you don't agree with the advice you're given and don't intend to implement it, thank people. Explicitly let them know that you value their perspective—because it's the same as saying you value *them*.
  - Instead of: "I know, I know."
  - Say: "Wow, I actually never thought of it that way before."
- **Be comfortable seeking help.** People who routinely ask for help—even if it's just in small and ordinary ways—communicate to others that they are
  - Humble

- Secure in themselves and accepting of their weaknesses
- Active problem solvers (yes, asking for help is a valid problem-solving strategy!)
- Able to collaborate and taking direction
- Open to learning
- Resourceful
- Able to value other people's contributions. Basically, a person who can ask for help is signaling a pro-social attitude, and will instantly be perceived as more likeable, down-to-earth and trustworthy. People who ask for help are team players.

Action step: If you want people to like you and trust you, it's almost always better to ask for advice than to give it. Is there someone in your world right now that would love the opportunity to share something valuable with you? Ask them their advice.

Be a conformist... but not when it really matters

Misconception 4: *Going along with the crowd is a bad idea. You should never follow others, but instead be a free and independent thinker.*

If your goal is to be well-liked and socially successful, should you be a nonconformist or should you go along with the crowd?

Deutsch & Gerard (1955) believe that it's important to first define *social influence*, and according to them, there are really two main kinds:

1. **Normative Influence**—When we conform to the group specifically because we want to be liked and accepted—*this is the desire to be liked.*

2. **Informational Influence**—When we conform to the group because we think that others are right about something, and we want to be right, too—*this is the desire to be right.*

Deutsch & Gerard were interested in how these types of influence affected a person's judgment and perception. By measuring participants' conformity behavior in different conditions, the researchers were able to observe that:

- When behavior was in public, people tended to be driven to act by normative influences and conform (even if they disagreed privately).
- When people were genuinely uncertain about the correct answer, they tended to be driven by informational influence.

So much for the different types of conformity, and the reasons why people might conform... but what about those people who resist the group?

Here we can turn to more recent research. Skitka et al. (2005) found that **people who express**

moral convictions are often perceived as more authentic and respected, even if others disagree with them.

It's as though conformity is perceived as understandable and even desirable if it's in the interests of fitting in, maintaining social harmony, and getting along with others. It's perhaps also viewed as socially reasonable to conform when experts or authorities are assumed to have superior or more comprehensive knowledge about something than we ourselves can. Here, conformity is shorthand for "staying informed."

Conformity, then isn't a bad thing. But there may be an exception: *moral convictions.*

A person who believes in something so completely that they will behave in ways that risk their approval from the group? This may actually signal:

- Courage
- Resilience
- Authenticity
- Trustworthiness

To finish, we'll consider the work of Moscovici (1969), which shows that **consistent minorities can influence majority opinion over time**. In other words, peer pressure can sometimes go the other way, and a minority can actually influence the majority—provided they are *consistent and firm* in their position.

The takeaway here:

- For things that are not that important, it's probably worth going with the crowd—or at least appearing to do so in public!
- It's OK to disagree and refuse to conform—but do so in a strategic way. Take a stand on things that you have strong moral convictions on, and be unwavering. People may not agree with you, but they will respect your integrity.
  - Calm, consistent disagreement over moral convictions always beats inconsistent conformity over insignificant issues
- Be mindful of group norms and be aware of when and *why* you're conforming. To be liked? To be right? Conforming isn't wrong—but do so consciously, and on your own terms.
  - **Before conforming for social approval, consider:** You may want to be accepted by a certain group, but *first qualify them*. Are they the kind of people you truly want to impress, emulate, and be influenced by?
  - **Before conforming for informational reasons, consider:** Is there really reason to believe that this group possesses knowledge you cannot otherwise

acquire? Sometimes, a little responsible research and critical thinking can help you identify your own position more clearly.
- **Likeability is sometimes about fitting in, and sometimes it's about standing out.** Decide where you want to lead, and where you're happy to follow. Choose which hills you're willing to die on… and which are ultimately not that important.

Action step: Though you may never be called to demonstrate them, what are your absolute, non-negotiable moral convictions? When it comes down to it, what *really* matters? Once you've identified these things, you can be a little more flexible in the rest. *Conscious conformity* can make life easier, more relaxed, and more harmonious.

Keep conversationally balanced

Misconception 5: There are two variations:

- *A good conversation is where you mostly listen, and let the other person do the bulk of the talking.*
- *A good conversation is where you get to talk a lot, and have other people listen to you*

There's a cruel irony that sometimes comes with being socially anxious. Do you know about it? It's called *talking too much*.

In your nervousness, you may rush to fill in silences, tell stories, crack jokes, or say something interesting.

You panic.

Then you do too much.

Sometimes we need to stop, take a breath. and remember that it's not about saying the "right thing" but making sure we're finding a dynamic balance between talking and listening.

But what *is* that balance? How much should we be talking?

In a real-world study (Sandstrom et al., 2016), researchers used smartphone sensors to track 473 everyday conversations. In the researcher's own words:

> "We tested whether conversational properties (conversation length, rate of turn taking, proportion of speaking time) and acoustical properties (volume, pitch) could predict enjoyment of a conversation. Surprisingly, **people enjoyed their conversations more when they spoke a smaller proportion of the time.**"

In the moment, talking a lot can feel like the right thing, and it can seem like conversational success to talk and be heard. Yet the results were clear: After conversations, those who actually talked more tended to report that they enjoyed themselves less.

So—talking too much is probably a bad idea. But does that mean we should be super quiet, nod, smile, and just listen most of the time? Let's see what else we can learn from the research.

A study published in *Personality and Social Psychology Bulletin* (Hirschi et. al., 2022) explained two important biases when it comes to conversational balance:

- **Bias 1: The reticence bias.** Defined by the authors as "the incorrect belief that they will be more likable if they speak less than half the time in a conversation with a stranger."
- **Bias 2: Halo ignorance.** Defined by the authors as "the belief that their speaking time should depend on their goal (e.g., to be liked vs. to be found interesting)."

The researchers devised studies to show that although these misconceptions are fairly widespread, people's predictions in this regard are almost always wrong. By randomly assigning people conversations where they would speak for 30%, 40%, 50%, 60%, or 70% of the time, they could measure people's actual ratings of how likeable they found their conversation partner.

They found that people tend to misjudge the ideal balance between talking and staying quiet.

Long story short: people are more likely to be rated as likeable when they speak *at least half the time* in conversations.

Holding back may feel polite or considerate, or you may keep quiet just because you're trying to avoid saying the wrong thing. But being too reserved has significant downsides:

- When you don't contribute much, you may end up communicating disinterest, disengagement, or even judgment.
- When you don't share yourself, people might perceive that you are not enjoying the conversation, and hence not enjoying *them.*
- By staying quiet, you inadvertently make the other person responsible for carrying the conversation.

OK, so to recap:

- We tend to enjoy conversations where we over speak far less than we think we will.
- It's possible to speak too little, too.

Try to stay balanced. Aim for:

50% listening and 50% talking *on average.*

Sometimes it will be 60% listening and 40% talking.

Sometimes it will be 40% listening and 60% talking.

It may shift constantly.

But *on average* it should be fairly evenly-split.

Try not to go outside those parameters, and attempt to *avoid either speaking or listening more than 60% of the time.*

This way, you are present, engaged, and participating, but you're also making space for the other person, which will boost your trustworthiness and likeability in their eyes, not to mention make the conversation more enjoyable for *you*.

A few rules of thumb:

- **This is just a representative figure.** At certain points, you'll speak more, and at certain points, they will. Sometimes the back-and-forth will be short and rapid fire, other times each person will take a longer turn to share. Take a mid- and long-term view and just ensure that overall, you both have the same amount of airtime.
- **Keep it fair.** A balanced conversation is not just about time spent talking, but about the *quality* of what's said. "Conversational risk" should be balanced, too—feed the conversation by disclosing something personal,

expressing an opinion, or making a claim, and invite them to do the same. It's not fair to ask others to give of themselves while we hold back.
- **Allow yourself to get excited.** Sometimes, in an effort to be a good listener, we can slip into "therapy mode" where we hope that, if we just center the other person and make them feel good, they'll like us. The opposite is true! Don't worry too much about being excitable, opinionated, or even accidentally interrupting people sometimes—the overall message is: "I'm enjoying this. Our conversation is engaging to me." That's a good thing!

Keep track of the overall give-and-take in a conversation and be aware of the flow.

Have you been speaking for a solid 5 minutes? Time to button it.

Have you shared your opinion or made a comment? Time to volley that ball back over to their side of the net by asking them a question.

Action step: Social anxiety can make us overly cautious and self-censor. Is the conversation lulling a little? It may be your turn to inject some life into it. Be forthcoming! Conversation is like a tennis match—the fun is in the back-and-forth. Launch something exciting over the net and see what happens.

Chapter 8: The romance element

The secret to an attractive online dating profile

The conventional understanding is that if you want a dating profile to stand out, it's all about the pictures, right?

Maybe not.

In a recent paper on the topic, (van der Zanden at. Al., 2022), the authors put forward what they believe is the most significant characteristic of an attractive dating profile: **originality**.

Being attractive absolutely matters—but there are many, many ways to be attractive, and physical attractiveness is just one.

It turns out that originality in dating profile text is perceived as pretty appealing, and another reliable way to be seen as attractive.

The obvious question is, what counts as *originality*?

- Being novel

- Being unusual or unexpected
- Being a little different from the norm
- Showing creativity and intelligence
- Showing independent thought
- Showing humor
- Appearing fresh
- Being unique
- Appearing authentic and genuine
- Capturing attention and being interesting

Originality means that we ourselves are the origin of what we are presenting meaning we aren't presenting something second-hand or fake.

In the art world, the originality of a work is whatever distinguishes it from copies or forgeries. An original is not derivative and is never a copy—if anything, it's what other people make copies *of!*

In general, the more original a profile, the better the impression it will make.

Originality = Effort + Personality

There are two components here:

- Personality – try to showcase the truly unique parts of yourself.
- Effort – showcase the fact that you have actually made an effort to present yourself well.

Particularly in the dating world, there is a long-standing misconception that obvious effort is somehow unattractive, and that we need to conceal effort and make our presentation seem nonchalant and almost accidental.

The truth is this can be incredibly off-putting for others!

The trick here is to **find balance.**

Being clever and creative is good, but don't go out of your way to be weird or it can backfire. Remember, you are not mimicking someone else's idea of a good profile, but generating your own.

If you're stumped about how to do this, consider the following:

- **Show your personality**. The authors found that *stylistic originality* was important—it's not just what you say, but how you say it.
    - Be specific. Give plenty of colorful little details and use vivid imagery and metaphors to paint a rich, totally unique picture.
    - Self-disclose, i.e., share something about yourself. You don't need to be inappropriate or blurt out all your secrets, just think about the things that make you you, and try to capture that in a few pithy statements that make you stand out from everyone else.

- **Demonstrate effort.**
  - Proofread! Error-free and properly composed writing shows that you're paying attention and that you care. And that's attractive.
  - Take the time to do things properly. Complete your profile, add quality, well-chosen pictures, and stay away from lazy cliches.

Originality is demonstrated in both the actual content and meaning of what you're sharing, but also in *how* you present it.

A few more tips:

- **Take your time**. A great dating profile is a work of art, so don't be surprised if it takes many hours to compile, and goes through many versions and iterations!
- **Get help.** Ask people who know you best to read your draft and give feedback. Ask them, "does this profile show *my uniqueness* as a person?" Remember you're not aiming for a generic "good profile", but an original one.
- **Do a little research.** Check out other people's profiles and find those that really strike you. Of course, don't copy them, but ask yourself why they work so well, and see what that principle looks like applied to your own personality.
- **Don't go crazy.** Finally, bear in mind the authors' final words: a good profile is "a

balancing act between novelty and appropriateness." Be creative, but don't push any buttons or break any obvious rules. You don't have to be controversial to be original.

Action step: Make a list of five things that would completely set you apart from a crowd of millions. Even if you're not creating a dating profile, think carefully about some easy and straightforward ways you can drop these little details into everyday conversation. The more specific, the better.

"What sounds beautiful is good"

Socially uncomfortable people often have a worry: "What am I going to say?!"

It may be more helpful to worry about *how* they're going to say it, though!

It's no surprise that people read voices in just the same way as they read body language, gestures, and facial expression. The voice is, in a way, a part of your body, and as much an expression of who you are as a person as any other characteristic.

In fact, research shows that the sound of a person's voice sends strong signals about that person's:

- Confidence levels
- Trustworthiness
- Physical attractiveness

- Age
- State of mind
- Even general health

This really shouldn't be surprising. Each of us generates our voice using our lungs, our voice boxes, and countless other organs of speech.

Speech that's shallow, breathy, gasping and light? That's a person who's feeling rushed and anxious.

Speech that's deep, low, and booming, or else small, high pitched, and delicate? This tells us about the literal size of the body making that noise—big or small, respectively.

Speech that's labored, unclear, or slurring? The body making that voice may be unhealthy or compromised in some way.

One study has shown that people really do perceive certain voices as more attractive than others—*and those first impressions are lightning fast.*

In fact the title of one fascinating paper—"What sounds beautiful is good: The vocal attractiveness stereotype"—reveals the innate bias most of us have for a nice-sounding voice (Zuckerman & Driver, 1989).

So, what *is* a nice-sounding voice?

Again, there are no surprises here:

For men – Voices rated as most attractive tend to be on the deeper side, potentially because they signal strength and a larger body size.

For women – Voices rated as most attractive tended to be higher pitched than men (but only *slightly*; extremely high-pitched voices are not rated as attractive). The authors supply a Shakespeare quote for the ideal feminine voice: "Her voice was ever soft, gentle, and low, an excellent thing in woman" (King Lear, Act V, Sc. 3). A testament perhaps to how unchanging certain preferences really are!

For both men and women – Clear, smooth, and expressive is almost always seen as more attractive than garbled, rough, or monotone.

Want a more attractive voice?

- If you're a woman, *slightly* increase your pitch and decrease your volume.
- If you're a man, *slightly* lower your pitch and increase your volume.
- Whether you're a man or a woman, pay attention to clear, articulate, and expressive speech that is smooth and enjoyable to listen to:
    - **Think *open*** – Straighten and unclench your posture, breathe fully and with your diaphragm, and relax your jaw and throat.
    - **Slow down** – A sure but unhurried pace signifies composure and confidence. Take

the time you need and deliver your words intentionally.
- **Relax** – Tight muscles and constricted airways will reveal themselves in your voice, and often sound unpleasant. You'll be able to enunciate with more clarity if you're loose, warm, and relaxed.
- **Use variety** – Let your voice be flexible and limber; if you gently move the pitch up and down, and vary your intonation, pitch and volume, you'll bring more vitality and color to your expression.

Your voice is uniquely yours, but there is a lot you can do to make it more appealing.

- Listen to audio books and notice how trained professionals modulate their expression. Notice their speed, pacing, and articulation. Practice reading out loud yourself.
- Before socializing, warm up your vocal cords, and imagine you're dressing them up for a party. It may feel silly, but try rehearsing a little out loud so you're ready to go.
- Be honest about any annoying vocal habits you have. Avoid talking too nasally, whining, "uptalk" (the so-called valley girl accent), vocal fry (Google it!), using too many "ums" and "uhs", excessive swearing, lip-smacking, or speed talking.

Vocal attractiveness is linked to personality perception. That means that if you are mindful of the way you're speaking, you may convince people to see you as friendly, confident, and competent *even if you actually aren't.*

Though it's not fair, we humans tend to make snap judgments about people's characters based on first impressions that are often no longer than a few milliseconds. The good news is that if you consciously leverage those first impressions, you can ensure you're perceived as more likeable in any social interaction.

A warning for those who are dating online or encountering others digitally before they do so face-to-face: Ratings for attractiveness tend to be rather high when based on only the voice or only the image, i.e., a photograph. People tend to form more modest opinions of overall attractiveness when presented with voice and image simultaneously.

What does this suggest?

Meet people in person as soon as possible, to prevent the possibility of them discovering that you are actually *less* attractive in person than your voice or photo would suggest!

Action step: Take up singing, public speaking, or even something like acting or standup comedy. Your voice is an instrument; the better you can get at using it skillfully, the more you'll get out of it.

Be proud, not arrogant

Many of us—especially women—have been indoctrinated with the belief that nobody likes a bragger.

If you want people to like you, then don't be arrogant, don't boast, and don't put yourself above others. In the dating context especially, most of us would say that a big ego is a big turnoff, right?

Actually, research by Shariff and Tracy (2009) finds that this is not the whole truth—although **it's important to distinguish the difference between authentic pride and mere arrogance.**

The researchers gathered participants from two very different cultures:

- Fijians (who ordinarily discourage open displays of status)
- North Americans (who ordinarily tolerate a little prideful boasting)

Using what's called implicit association tasks (IATs), the researchers tested people's automatic reactions to displays of pride and status, and the associations they make when viewing someone make "displays of status."

Let's quickly clarify what a "display of status" refers to in this study: it's a *nonverbal* expression of pride, for example:

- Puffing out the chest a little
- Putting arms akimbo, expansive posture
- Standing tall
- Lifting the chin high / tilting the head back
- A self-satisfied expression

The results of the IATs showed that in both the Fiji and American groups, **"pride expressions" were associated with high status.**

The researcher's interpreted it this way: Pride expressions have actually played an important evolutionary role in negotiating hierarchies in social groups in humans. In other words, such displays are accurate signals of status, competence, and worth—and allow the signaler to convey this status without it causing conflict.

The researchers found that this effect was stable across all cultures. Even the Fijians, who officially discourage status displays, showed automatic responses not much different from their North American counterparts.

Here's the rub:

There's a difference between implicit and explicit perception of prideful displays in other people:

- Implicit – what you actually think
- Explicit – what you say and how you behave

The Fijians discourage overt self-promotion in their culture, yet at the same time, they still respond to a pride display as a signal of status. They *explicitly* condemn pride displays but *implicitly* respond to them as though they were genuine signals.

What can we take from all this?

Generally, prideful nonverbal expression is a universal status cue—regardless of what the cultural explicitly claims.

If you display subtle signals of being proud of yourself, people tend to take your word for it and treat this display as a genuine mark of status. For those of us who struggle socially, this offers an amazing shortcut and lends support for the old advice to **fake it till you make it.**

In social situations:

- **Be aware of your body.** You might just be comfortable and relaxed, but if you're slumped or slouched, you may be unconsciously perceived as cowering or low status.
- **Keep it nonverbal.** This research is about nonverbal status displays—body language and posture—*not* verbal bragging and boasting.
- **Tread carefully.** A prideful display may give you a slight status boost, but there can still be some cultural trade-offs. Even

if people do perceive you as high status, they may still publicly disapprove or penalize you in some other way.
- **Be authentic.** Being prideful in a way that is perceived as undeserved could backfire and decrease your likeability. Express pride around activities where you have a genuine "right" to feel competent or competent, otherwise it may be seen as *hubris*.
- **Context matters.** Generally, displays of pride are more appropriate and more effective in professional contexts, leadership situations, or when a genuine competition or contest is underway. People who show authentic pride *after* a success are seen as more competent, respected, and likeable.
- **Lose the faux humility.** There's no need to downplay your wins or stifle genuine feelings of satisfaction and pride out of fear that people will find it unlikeable. Be subtle, enjoy your success, stand tall, and convey a sense of calm certainty—not conceit. It will make you *more* appealing, not less.
- **Honestly recognize others' status, too.** When someone does well, respond positively and affirm their success—this not only strengthens your bond and shows support, but it also makes *you* look

supremely confident and secure. It's a win-win!

Action step: Watch your posture. Stand tall, keep your chin up, pull your shoulders back. Even if you feel ultra-confident, slouching and stooping sends all the wrong messages. Stand up straight and you instantly appear higher status.

Tweak the recipe

The poets of the world have grappled with it extensively, but scientifically speaking, what *is* love? What is it made of?

According to American psychologist Robert Sternberg's Triangular Theory of Love (1986), romantic love is a known quantity made up of three key ingredients:

- **Intimacy** – Feeling close, bonded, connected; the presence of affection, understanding, and care.
- **Passion** – Physical attraction, sexual desire, chemistry.
- **Commitment** – The repeated and conscious decision to sustain the relationship.

For Sternberg, the wide range of different types of relationships could all be understood in terms of their ratio of these three key ingredients. Here are a few "recipes" for different love or relationship types:

- **Non-love** – That is, zero on all three ingredients.
  - A stranger or even enemy.
- **Liking** – High intimacy (closeness, bonding) but zero passion and varying commitment levels.
  - Higher commitment makes a good friend; lower levels are associated with moderate friends or acquaintances.
- **Infatuation** – High, often sudden, passion, but low commitment and intimacy.
  - Often called *limerence*, this blend can indicate a serious crush or obsession with someone you don't actually know—in extremes, a "parasocial" relationship with a celebrity or influencer, or a potential stalker situation!
- **Empty love** – High commitment but no intimacy or passion.
  - Can be seen in arranged marriages, marriages where divorce is not an option, or the "staying together for the kids" situation.
- **Romantic love** – High intimacy, high passion but relatively little commitment.
  - This is a very early dating relationship or a passionate but tenuous love affair.
- **Companionate love** – High intimacy and high commitment, but low or zero passion.
  - Think of very long-term relationships or those between older people.

- **Fatuous love** – High commitment and high passion, but low intimacy (relatively rare!).
  - Imagine a whirlwind lusty affair followed by a sudden marriage—skipping out on the emotional intimacy part.
- **Consummate love** – The ideal form, according to Sternberg anyway. A balanced, complete mix of all three.
  - A happy marriage where the couple is physically affectionate, emotionally bonded, and also deeply committed.

Adult friendships and romantic relationships can be confusing because it's sometimes difficult to know which is which!

People can enter into "situationships" where expectations are unclear, uncommunicated, or even unknown to themselves.

- One person considers the other a best friend, while the other thought they were acquaintances at best.
- Two people hang out for years only to realize that one of them sincerely thought they were dating.
- Someone says, "We should hang out sometime" and is surprised and a little annoyed when the other person actually takes them up on the offer.

Sternberg's theory can help us draw clear lines between relationship types. The clearer you can be about how each of your relationships measure on these three components, the less you'll have to handle awkward misunderstandings like the above!

Not only can the theory help you identify the parameters of a romantic relationship, but it can also serve as a kind of relationship diagnostic tool. For example:

- **Intimacy** – Friends share personal thoughts and feelings, exchange help and support, bond over mutual experiences, and feel emotionally in one another's "inner circle." Most romantic partners do the same.
  - Do I actually feel close to this person?
  - Do they know me? Do I know them?
- **Passion** – Friendships (should!) lack any sexual attraction, but that doesn't mean there isn't a platonic kind of chemistry: having fun together, genuinely enjoying one another's company, getting one another's jokes, and generally being on the same wavelength. In romantic relationships, the passion level needs to be mutually agreed upon.
  - Do I enjoy this person?
  - Do we have the same ideas and expectations around passion?
- **Commitment** – While people never make formal or public commitments to their friends, there is nevertheless an unspoken feeling that someone has decided to make the conscious effort and *choose* that

friendship, putting in the work to build and maintain trust and loyalty over time. In romantic relationships, commitment is usually a sign that relationship is intended to be serious and lasting.
- Have I actually decided that this person is my friend or partner? Have they made the same decision?
- How much work are we both willing to put in?

The liking relationship type is characterized primarily by *intimacy* and *commitment*. The presence of sexual passion immediately disqualifies it as a friendship and places it in another category entirely.

Friendships *can* morph into other relationship types—like romantic, companionate or consummate love—but only those types where intimacy is also present.

Likewise, other relationship types can morph into friendships, but again only if intimacy is present. Many couples learn this the hard way when they break up and try to "stay friends"—only to discover that they were never really friends in the first place, and that once passion and commitment are removed, the lack of real intimacy is evident.

If you're in a romantic relationship:

- **Appraise**. Ask yourself how the connection measures up in terms of intimacy, passion, and commitment.
- **Align**. Check that you and the other person have the same assumptions, desires, and expectations about those three key ingredients
- **Action**. If something isn't working, identify which of the three components may be lacking, and take action there.

The triangular theory of love applied to friendship

- There are many types of relationship, but great friendships are always characterized by *high intimacy*, *high platonic chemistry*, and *commitment*.
- If a friendship is fizzling, flopping, or failing to launch, take a look at which of these components might be missing.

Want to deepen a friendship? There are only really two ways: increase intimacy or increase commitment.

How do you increase intimacy?

Be around one another! Spend time together. Over time, gradually reveal a little more about yourself, and invite the other person to open up with thoughtful questions and genuine listening. Find something you share in common or engineer a new challenge or adventure you can face together. Slowly ratchet up trust by revealing your deeper thoughts and feelings, asking advice, or offering support, kindness, and validation.

How do you increase commitment?

Demonstrate your willingness to maintain and cultivate the relationship. Make an effort. Invite them out, plan meetups and remember their birthday. Reach out and ask them questions. Stay in touch. Invest the time. Show up and show that you're in it for the long haul, even if it's just in small ways. What are their goals? Show an interest. Support them in whatever way you can. What are they struggling with? Show that you're there to help.

Action tip: Pick the three most important relationships in your life right now, and appraise each in terms of the three components. What does your appraisal tell you?

Communal vs. exchange relationships

Picture two scenarios:

1. You're on a lunch break with a colleague. You get on very well with this colleague and have collaborated with them for more than a decade. One day they forget their wallet at home so you offer to pay for their lunch. "Thanks!" they say. "I'll get your lunch tomorrow." The next day, you

notice that they are careful to buy you a meal of exactly equal value.
2. You're out in town one day with your spouse to whom you've been happily married for more than a decade. You walk past a shop front when suddenly they see something they fall in love with. You spontaneously decide to buy it for them. The next day, they present *you* with a gift. You notice the gift is of exactly the same value as the one you bought them yesterday.

Now, carefully consider both these scenarios. In both, there is a giving action by one party, followed by reciprocity in the other party.

Yet these two scenarios don't quite *feel* the same, do they?

If you're like most people, you might find the colleague's willingness to repay your kindness quite endearing, and like them more for it. Yet somehow, if your own spouse did the same thing, it would feel mildly... insulting.

According to Clark & Mills (1979), there's a reason for this, and it comes down to the fact that there are broadly two types of relationships:

- **Communal relationships** are those where giving is based on the other person's need, and there is no expectation of repayment. The aim is simply to meet that person's need, care for them, and uphold their wellbeing.

- **Exchange relationships are different.** These involves giving that occurs in the context of reciprocity—you give because that person gave to you before, or because you expect to receive a return in future. Here, the aim is to balance costs and benefits—to be *fair*.

Marriage is (or should be!) a communal relationship, whereas work colleagues tend to be exchange relationships. When you treat a communal relationship like an exchange relationship? Things feel awkward. There's a rupture.

Clark & Mills' experiments showed that:

- When someone repaid a favor after receiving one, it actually **decreased attraction** *when in the context of a communal relationship.*
- On the other hand, when someone repaid a favor after receiving one, it **increased attraction** *when in the context of an exchange relationship.*

To return to our example, reciprocity in our work colleagues makes us like them more, whereas reciprocity in the context of exchange from our spouse actually undermines our attraction for them.

The implications are interesting.

- **Pay careful attention to the relationship type.** The only way to judge the appropriateness of giving is to first determine how that giving will be interpreted. Be aware that one party could believe they're in a communal relationship while the other believes it's transactional!
- **In exchange relationships, play fair**. With neighbors, acquaintances, and people at work, it's better to promptly return favors and work on a principle of equal contribution. The Franklin Effect holds (i.e., people will like you more if you ask a favor of them) but in more superficial relationships, it's worth keeping these favors more or less balanced.
    - In exchange relationships, failure to reciprocate will feel like exploitation.
- **In communal relationships, don't keep score**. Closely tracking each person's contributions will actually reduce attraction, trust, and liking, and weaken the feeling of goodwill and genuine care. In such relationships, reciprocity actually creates awkwardness. This could be:
    - Asking for help, receiving it and then immediately finding ways to pay it back.

- Giving someone help, and then immediately asking them for a favor.

Action step: If you're dating as a woman, it may feel natural to want to "split the bill" on a first date or keep fairly even in the early days of dating. However, doing so may actually create a more transactional frame.

New relationships naturally start out more transactional and gradually become more communal. A date of either gender who insists on keeping close track of every little contribution is sending the message that they still see the connection in terms of transaction. Tread carefully.

Another tip: If you're attempting to extend a friendship with a colleague to beyond the office, you'll need to gradually shift from transactional to communal. Do small favors for them that you deliberately don't track and refuse any reciprocation. Then wait to see if they do the same.

Face-to-face is best

In an editorial introduction to a special issue in *Philosophical Transactions of the Royal Society B*, Hamilton and Holler's (2023) explored the art and science of face-to-face interaction.

The editorial begins, "Face-to-face interaction is core to human sociality and its evolution..." and, despite the ubiquity of online communication today, it's hard to argue with that.

The telephone was invented less than two hundred years ago, and widespread video calls have been available for less than thirty years. Before that, human bonding took place in one way and one way only: face to face.

Whether it's bonding, teaching, flirting, arguing, gossiping, joking, or comforting, **human beings have evolved to talk in person**, and close enough to hear one another's voices and see one another's faces.

Hamilton and Holler go so far as to say that face-to-face interaction has shaped every part of our social nature as a species, which has enormous implications for our health and wellbeing, and our evolution over time.

The researchers considered human communication on many levels. For our intents and purposes, however, a few interesting insights stand out:

- **Nonverbal communication matters.** Social interaction is so much more than just words, data, or content. Information is conveyed just as much through micro expressions, gestures, posture, vocal quality, and other body language cues.
- **The "perception of social presence" matters.** Feeling that there is truly someone

there, and that you're really engaged with them, is key. The authors find that social communication is more successful when people feel connected in this way.
- **Social cognition is complicated.** The authors find that nonverbal expression and social presence are not easily replicated, and play an important role in how we think, understand ourselves, and connect with others.

Basically, **much is lost when communication is taken online.** Though video calls allow a certain convenience, they also distort and weaken our ability to detect and respond to those all-important nonverbal cues.

Being physically present in the same environment, in other words **being embodied together**, has a profound and irreplaceable influence on human interaction.

Face-to-face interactions engage unique brain systems that aren't activated by digital or remote communication.

- You don't have a true, three-dimensional sense of the way the other person's body is moving and taking up space.
- You miss all those little eye movements, gestures, and subtle changes in posture and tone of voice.
- Not to mention the fact that you can't smell or touch them!

There is so, so much more to "read" in social interactions when they are alive, current, and fully immersive. Real life interaction is natural, information-rich, and dynamic.

Being physically co-present changes cognition and deepens understanding. The study calls for greater use of naturalistic, real-life interaction in social research.

- If you're online dating, meet offline as soon as possible. Zoom chats are helpful for staying connected in established relationships, but they'll seldom help you create new ones.
- If you have to connect digitally, make an extra effort to pay attention to nonverbal cues, and try to make your own cues more obvious. You may need to deliberately say out loud what you're thinking and feeling, since this information may not travel as well through the ordinary nonverbal channels.
- If you've spent a lot of time in online and digital spaces, try to find time for more naturalistic interactions, too. Even casual coffee shop chats or small talk with people at the supermarket can help you recalibrate.

Action step: Wherever possible choose face-to-face interactions. Face to face connection will always be more neurologically and emotionally impactful, more satisfying, and richer than digital or screen-based interaction.

Chapter 9: Becoming socially intelligent

Three types of social capital

Social skills are about so much more than dating, making friends or getting along with your family. The world is filled with people who can mutually offer one another all sorts of benefits—we often don't have the words to describe these kinds of relationships, however.

Enter the concept of social capital.

Social capital = relationships and networks that provide productive and cooperative *benefits*, for example favors, resources, or information.

Social capital is who you know. It's your "connections."

Basically, every person is embedded in a network of relationships with others, and all of those relationships can serve very different functions.

Knowing how to communicate well, to resolve conflict in romantic relationships, and to maintain peace in a family is one set of skills.

Knowing who to talk to, what strings to pull and which people to be nice to? That's an entirely different set of skills!

There is in fact an Institute for Social Capital, and in 2018 Tristan Claridge collaborated with them to offer a full conceptual model for thinking and talking about social capital.

In Claridge's model, there are three broad types of social capital:

- **Bonding Social Capital.**
    - This is friends and family.
    - Trust and connection are high.
    - Similarity is high.
    - *Purpose:* Members help one another "get by"—i.e., they support and help one another.
    - *Higher purpose:* Resilience.
- **Bridging Social Capital.**
    - This can include people in professional networks, and connections across different social groups.
    - People from different cultures, socio-economic groups, communities, religions, or backgrounds.
    - *Purpose:* Extends reach and influence, exploits new opportunities, and links wider networks. Members help one another "get ahead."
    - *Higher purpose:* Growth.
- **Linking Social Capital.**

- While the previous two types are *horizontal*, this type is *vertical*—it's connections to those with higher power and authority.
- It can include links to institutions, organizations, governments, and other influential bodies.
- *Purpose*: To secure access to resources, to exert influence, and affect decision-making, or to secure institutional support.
- *Higher purpose*: Power; Societal or institutional change.

While this may be an interesting framework, what does it mean for us?

There are several insights we can glean from Claridge's model:

- **Function and context matters.** Not all connections / relationships are the same, nor do they serve the same purpose. It's worth being aware of the overall function a connection is serving in your life, and your function to *them*. This will help you gain clarity about how to maintain that connection appropriately.
- **Be well-rounded.** Close friendships and family absolutely matter, but that's not all you need. Diversify your social network by seeking out and nurturing acquaintances from different

backgrounds as well as people in influential positions.
- **Consider the value you hold for others.** Where do you fit in other people's networks? You might not bond well with a person on a deep emotional level, but that doesn't mean you can't be mutually useful connections for one another.

Most people find it easier to maintain closeness with their nearest and dearest, and a little harder to reach out beyond that inner circle. But it's not as hard as it seems!

How can you be more socially intelligent?

Join a new group, reach out to a colleague or neighbor you wouldn't ordinarily think of connecting with, or volunteer locally to expose yourself to a wide range of different people. Remind yourself constantly that you don't have to be ultra-best friends with everyone for them to serve a function in your social network.

Also consider going to community or governmental meetings and attending town hall or school board meetings. Get to know who is in charge of what. Try faith-based or advocacy groups, and get involved with community organizations.

Network professionally and devise a system for keeping track of the people you meet—one of the best things you can do for your broader network is to consciously introduce people to one another. You never quite know how your favor will be repaid!

Action step: Any time a new person enters your world, quickly ascertain where they might fit in your social world. Learn a little about them, get their contact details and share details about yourself. You may not click emotionally, but these "weak connections" can prove extremely useful later on.

Keep it mutual

Picture this. You've met a new friend, and things look good—you're hanging out regularly, you enjoy one another's company and you're slowly getting to know one another better. Eventually, they meet your other friends, even members of your family. After some time, it feels pretty automatic to call this person your friend.

And yet one day, you discover that your friend had their birthday the weekend past... and you weren't invited.

Awkward!

Has this kind of thing ever happened to you?

In a 2016 paper by Almaatouq et. al., a group of researchers point out a truth that many of us take a while to realize: **Not all friendships are mutual**. In other words, just because we feel a certain way about someone, it doesn't necessarily mean that they feel the same way.

If you don't know someone well (by definition, you won't know new acquaintances very well!) or if you're not socially confident, it can be tricky to recognize when a friendship is a little lopsided.

- How well do you know this person?
- How much do you like them?
- Objectively, how close are you both?
- In a general sense, what do you *mean* to one another?

The sometimes awkward truth is that you and the other person may answer the above questions in very, very different ways.

Now, the interesting thing is that the paper's authors were not writing from the perspective of social scientists. They aren't psychologists, and they aren't interested in friendship at all but published their findings in *Social and Information Networks* for fellow computer scientists.

Their investigation was more about social contagions and how they spread through online social networks, as well as how new behaviors spread more easily through mutual friendships, rather than one-way friendships.

Basically, they found that when it comes to peer influence, *reciprocity* and *directionality* matter. One of the defining features of a mutual, balanced friendship? **People in mutual**

friendships are more likely to influence one another's behavior and respond to their encouragement or peer pressure.

The authors suggest that there is a difference between:

- Passive social learning (adopting the behaviors and preferences of those around you) and
- Active social persuasion that results in behaviors transferring from one friend to another.

Now, presuming you're not a social scientist interested in "designing interventions that seek to harness social influence for collective action", what does this mean for you?

We'll look at things from a different perspective: *if a person considers you a friend, they are more likely to change their behavior in response to pressure or encouragement from you.*

This gives you a convenient "test" or yardstick to check up on a growing friendship and see where you stand—hence avoiding the kind of awkwardness described earlier.

- **Make suggestions and observe how they respond.** Mention a fitness challenge, make recommendations for online retailers or service providers, share a tool or product you use, talk about a charity you volunteer for, mention an app you've signed up for or

an event you're going to. People may well be polite, but pay close attention to *the degree to which they seem willing to change their behavior* based on your suggestions. It will tell you a lot!
- **Keep it balanced.** It's easy to misjudge if a friendship is truly balanced, or moving at an even pace. Notice if you seem more willing to change your behavior on their account than vice versa. Pay attention to how many invitations and offers you're making compared to them—try always to be aware of their pace, interest, and tone, *and match it.*
- **Recognize and respect the influence you have on others.** If someone has gone out of their way to adjust their behavior on your account, recognize this as a sign of wanting to be closer to you.

Action step: Have you had a message go unanswered? An invite turned down? A suggestion or offer rebuffed? It's not the end of the world if there's more interest on your side than theirs. But it matters what you do next. Be patient, and allow closeness to develop organically, even if it's slower than you'd like. But it's also OK to have a hard limit, for example, "I never reach out more than three times in a row."

The ten social dimensions

Quick, think of the last three social interactions you had.

Chances are each of these interactions were quite different from one another, right?

Maybe you've noticed that when you're with one friend, it always leads to the same kind of conversation. Maybe time spent with another friend always takes on the same predictable vibe. Maybe it makes a lot of sense to do a certain activity with a certain friend, yet you can't begin to imagine doing that with a different friend.

Why?

Minje Choi and colleagues may have an interesting perspective that can help us understand and conceptualize what is actually happening when people get together socially and communicate.

Choi and colleagues conducted an enormous data study:

- They first annotated almost 10,000 conversational texts (including those found online) with a set of ten chosen dimensions, using a process called "crowd labelling."
- They then trained NLP models to analyze enormous data sets to predict which of the ten dimensions would appear in certain texts.
- The analyzed data included:
    - 160 million Reddit messages
    - 290,000 emails from the Enron corporation

- 300,000 lines of movie dialogue

The research team presented their observations at The Web Conference (WWW 2020).

So what did they find?

- They were able to accurately detect ten predictable "building blocks" for social relationships, using text alone.
- The exact mix of dimensions in any text exchange revealed a lot about the character of the relationship between the people communicating (for example supportive, romantic, conflictual, etc.).
- Certain dimensions were even found to be associated with real-world demographics, like income level, education, and even things like suicide rates.

The ten social dimensions or building blocks were:

1. Exchange of knowledge or information
2. Power dynamics (e.g. boss / employee)
3. Status giving (e.g. praise or gratitude)
4. Trust
5. Support
6. Romance
7. Similarity (i.e., homophily)

8. Identity (belonging and group membership)
9. Fun
10. Conflict

The researchers believe that all social interactions can be accurately described using just these ten building blocks, in varying proportions.

These researchers were primarily interested in language-based profiling, and ways to accurately understand social dynamics based on text alone. This would allow them, for example, to build better online communication platforms or improve the way that social media works.

But how can we apply this insight to our own (offline) social lives?

The value of a study like this is that it gives us *clarity* and *precision*. It allows us to take a close look at social interactions and clearly see all the elements that go into them.

Try this:

1. After every conversation or social interaction, ask yourself, **"Which social dimensions were present? Which were absent?"** You could even visualize a spider graph or chart to map out the relative proportions, bearing in mind

that the goal is not to have all of them present to the max!
2. Next, ask yourself how you might consciously shift this balance. If you're happy with an interaction, then obviously you don't need to make changes. But if not, **reflect and consider which dimension you could have amplified, and which you could have reduced.**
3. The next time you engage with this person, **consciously change your language** to cue and activate certain dimensions. Don't forget to listen actively and consider the cues they're sending, and the dimensions they're favoring.

For example, if you find that conversations with a certain friend always take a turn for the competitive (*conflict*, *power dynamics*) then you may consciously adjust your language to bring in more *fun*, *status giving,* or *similarity*.

Instead of subtly one-upping one another or boasting, you can be more playful and humorous, use "we" language or draw attention to all the ways you and this friend are actually similar, and on the same team.

Small language tweaks make a big difference!

Things will *feel* different. The other person won't be able to put their finger on it, but you'll know why!

Being emotionally intelligent is not some vague, mysterious magic or unexplained phenomenon—it's as simple as taking charge of the language you use and *intentionally* choosing to cultivate closeness, likability, connection, and understanding.

Action step: Think of someone in your world right now that you're experiencing a little conflict, misunderstanding or friction with. Ask: Which of the ten social dimensions are at play? And which would you have to introduce to bring more harmony? Identify one or two social dimensions, and then find simple ways to change your language accordingly to start cultivating that element.

Don't be responsible, be responsive

Sometimes, when you're socially anxious, it can feel like the success of the interaction rests entirely on your shoulders. You may feel enormous pressure to "say the right thing" and come up with something that is:

- Interesting
- Amusing
- Impressive
- Intelligent
- Novel
- Attractive

But while you're stressing over all this responsibility, you may have missed something important: There is another person in the conversation, and what unfolds between you is 50% down to *them*!

Instead of focusing on the statements you make, remind yourself to **ask questions.** Recognize the value of their contribution and invite it.

In conversations, questions serve a range of different functions all at once:

- They show the other person that you're actually paying attention.
- They demonstrate that you care about what you're hearing.
- They keep the dynamic, back-and-forth flow alive.
- Not to mention they take the pressure off of you!

In a paper titled, "It Doesn't Hurt to Ask: Question-Asking Increases Liking" Huang et al. (2017) explain how asking a question is always a good move, but some kinds of questions are extra-effective at creating rapport and liking.

Across three different studies, these researchers found that **people who asked plenty of *follow up questions* were rated as more likable.**

It makes sense. If you merely ask a string of rapid-fire, unconnected questions, that's not a conversation. It's an interview (or an interrogation!).

But follow-up questions signal genuine *responsiveness*. They communicate: "I'm here. I'm listening. I understand you. And I care about what you've just said so much that I'd like to know more."

The funny thing is, most of us don't truly understand just how powerful follow-up questions can be. Huang and colleagues found that people almost always underestimated the positive effects of follow up questions, highlighting a surprising mismatch between our social intuition and reality.

When it comes to being perceived as likable, it really doesn't matter much how many interesting, attractive, or intelligent things you can think of to say. **What does matter? Being able to demonstrate responsiveness.**

Be present.

Listen.

Respond in ways that show you are receptive, alert, and engaged.

Show interest and care for what you're told by deliberately asking for more information.

One of the most flattering things you can do for people is to not only signal that you are hearing, understanding and enjoying the message they're sending, but also that you'd like to hear even more.

By some strange communication alchemy, people tend to most like those that make *them* feel heard, seen, understood, valued, and connected with.

So what does a good follow up question look like?

- **Keep it simple.** Grab a hold of a single detail you've heard and ask for more detail—use "5W and a H" questions (who, what, when, where, why and how). For example:
  - "I come from a huge family—we were seven kids in total."
  - "Oh wow! That's huge. So what number were you?"
  - "I was number 4!"
  - "Ha, right in the middle. What was that like growing up?"
- **Start with a comment, reaction, or expression.** People like to know that their message has "landed" and that, in some small way, others have been affected by what they've shared.
  - "Really!? That's crazy."
  - "Unbelievable."
  - "Thank goodness."
  - "Uh oh..."
- **Stay balanced**. Generally, you should ask a lot more follow-up questions than you think. Aim for a *maximum of around three in a row*, before you shift back to yourself or make a statement of your own.

- **Listen for the emotion.** Follow up questions open up a conversation and help it take shape according to any number of possible threads. If you want to build connection and closeness, listen for cues that certain details hold more emotion for the speaker—then ask a follow-up question about *that*.
  - Do they suddenly seem more animated and energetic when they talk about a certain topic? Pick up on that and ask them to elaborate—it's an easy way to bring vitality and energy into a conversation.
  - On the other hand, occasionally you might want to steer a conversation *away* from emotional topics, for example in professional contexts or where romantic interest is not reciprocated. Ask follow-up questions about the most neutral parts of their message instead!

Tip: Are you afraid of coming across as too nosy or asking too many questions? Follow this format to get all the benefits of follow-up questioning, but without sabotaging the natural flow of the interaction:

Excellent responsiveness = reaction or expression + small self-disclosure + follow-up question.

For example: "No way! I've always dreamed of winning the lottery. I'm super curious, what was the first thought that popped into your mind when you realized?"

This way, in one short response, you are demonstrating your attention and presence, staying balanced, and keeping the conversational flow going without things feeling too obvious or effortful.

However, you don't have to follow any specific formula if you can simply maintain a genuine attitude of curiosity. If you're ever unsure, just say, "Ooh, tell me more..." Paired with open body language, eye contact and an attitude of sincere curiosity, you can't go wrong.

Action step: Practice the "responsiveness formula" above in your next social interaction, and take notes. One handy trick is just to paraphrase and echo back what you're told in a question form. "We're now looking for property in Canada." Response: "Oh wow, you're actually thinking of buying a house in Canada?" Done.

The secret to applied empathy

Picture this: You've just heard the best news of your life, and you're full to the brim with excitement and happiness. You're just bursting to tell someone, and so you call up a friend and start gushing on the phone. You enthusiastically tell them every amazing detail, and when you eventually pause for breath, they say,

"Oh. That's cool."

Then silence.

Your friend then eventually says, "Oh by the way, I confirmed the meetup with Jenny tomorrow."

Oof. Hear that? It's the sound of all your excitement and joy instantly deflating.

What is it exactly that's so wrong about this exchange?

Like Huang and colleagues, you can probably see that the thing that's missing is **responsiveness**. But according to Harry T. Reis and colleagues (2010), there are particular situations in which we need to provide a very particular *kind* of responsiveness.

In a study paper titled, "Are you happy for me? How sharing positive events with others provides personal and interpersonal benefits", Reis et. al., explore the phenomenon of sharing positive events—and how the people in our lives respond to our good news.

Broadly, when someone tells us their good news, our response can vary according to:

- Whether it's **active or passive** – do we supply effort, energy, and intention, or not?
- Whether it's **constructive or destructive** – does it build up connection or break it down?

This yields four possible response types:

- **Active constructive** – We respond with energy, enthusiasm, and warmth. We affirm the importance and significance of the news, and mirror the teller's emotional state. We show appreciation, joy, support, gratitude, or pleasant surprise.
    - Example: "Wow! That's so amazing! Congratulations, I'm so pleased for you!" (paired with nonverbal body language that reflects theirs).
- **Passive constructive** – We respond in a positive but low energy and low effort way.
    - Example: "Good for you."
- **Active destructive** – We respond in a way that negates, undermines, or otherwise contradicts the good news, but in a more deliberate way.
    - Example: "OK calm down, it's not that big a deal."
- **Passive destructive** – We negate and undermine the good news via our lack of attention, enthusiasm, or care.
    - Example: "Yeah, I had the same thing happen to me last year. Hey, can you pass the remote?"

It goes without saying that **it's responses that are both *active* and *constructive* that are more associated with feelings of closeness, validation, and trust.**

Though many of us know we need to be kind and understanding when people are feeling bad, we might be less familiar with the opposite skill—what to do when they're feeling really good!

It turns out that our ability to empathize with positive feelings may reveal more about the health, intimacy, and trust levels in our relationship. Why? Because it's a genuine signal that we care about that person's wellbeing, and are invested in their happiness and good fortune *even if it has nothing to do with us.*

When a person feels that we feel this way about them, it creates a deep impression of trust.

When we are responsive, we receive the entirety of the other person's message—and that means **responding and reacting to the emotional content** of what they're sharing. Sure, *we* may not exactly feel their excitement or joy, but we demonstrate that we've heard their excitement, validate it, and care enough to reflect that back to them.

Bottom line: if you want people to like you, and feel safe and happy around you, respond with enthusiasm and warmth to their good news—even and especially when that news does not benefit you in any way.

Celebrate others' wins like they're your own.

Action step: We can apply this principle in reverse, too. Think carefully about your current friendships. Though some people may appear empathetic if they tend to us in our misery, it's really those who can celebrate with us in our joy that are true friends.

Chapter 10: The habits of the socially successful

Practice small acts of reliability

When most people consider how they can improve their social skills, they readily think of being more likeable, ramping up the charm, gaining confidence, or learning better conversation skills.

But something almost nobody thinks about? Your *trustworthiness*.

Being trustworthy might not seem very glamorous or exciting, until you realize that relationships of all kinds crash and burn without it.

But what is trust?

When a person trusts something or someone, it's an attitude they hold—they believe in the reliability, truth, or capability of something or someone. **To be trustworthy, then, is to inspire and elicit these feelings of trust—to make yourself a person that other people can rely on and believe in.**

Author and professor of psychology Eli Finkel believes that trust is not just one thing, but *three* separate things. Writing for the Kellogg School of Management, Finkel explains:

- **Predictability** – Confidence that the other person will behave in consistent and expected ways.

- **Dependability** – Belief that the other person will act to sustain your wellbeing when you need it, *even when it doesn't benefit them personally.*

- **Faith** – The conviction that the other person will stick around even if things get difficult.

Now, although Finkel mainly refers to marriages and romantic relationships, the same three components can really be found in any relationship, big or small, shallow or deep.

Finkel draws particular attention to this part: We trust those we can depend on to care about us *even when it doesn't benefit them personally.*

He calls these **diagnostic situations**—i.e., those times when we can clearly observe someone acting in our interests

- Even when they don't *have* to
- And even when doing so inconveniences them or works against their own interests.

These moments are "diagnostic" because they sort the wheat from the chaff, so to speak: they are an honest signal that someone could easily have not cared, but chose to anyway. This separates those who are kind out of convenience, from those who you can truly trust.

The great thing about seeing trust in this way is that it allows you to uncover the mechanism by which trust is actually built up—and then deliberately build up trust, one step at a time.

Trust is earned, gradually.

Intimacy with other people always entails risk. After all, the closer you are, the more hurt you will be should that person do something to harm you.

However, by a series of mutual tests and confirmations, each party in a new relationship can gradually feel out the other—not all at once, but by a series of reciprocal gestures that gradually ratchet up trust.

Trust is a process, and it goes like this:

1. You take a tiny step towards intimacy, and willingly incur a tiny emotional risk.
2. The other person sees that tiny risk you willingly took, and chooses to respect and honor it. They *could* hurt you, but they choose not to. In fact, in return, they may even take the same emotional risk you just did.
3. You see them deliberately choosing not to hurt you despite having the opportunity,

and this is one tiny data point that says: This person might be OK. You might be able to trust them.

Every time someone takes an emotional risk with you, and you acknowledge, respect and reciprocate it, trust is built.

The wonderful thing about trust is that it can be built from teeny, tiny things.

Small moments of reliability, little gestures of dependability, and everyday acts that demonstrate that you care, even when you don't have to... these things add up.

It's great to be likeable, but if you want to be trustworthy, find ways to be consistently reliable, predictable and dependable:

- **Be punctual.** If you say you're going to be somewhere at a certain time, be there. People may not even consciously register such a thing, but they'll nevertheless emotionally register you as someone who keeps their word. Someone who can be expected to do what they say they will. Be the person that always follows through. That's always going to be an appealing quality in a person, no matter the relationship you have with them.
- **Don't flake.** Life happens and sometimes the unexpected means you have to cancel commitments, but as far as possible, don't

pull out at the last minute or leave people hanging.
- **Tell the truth.** Being perceived as honest is about more than just not lying. Be impeccable with your word. No little white lies, exaggerations or fudging the truth. Don't let people see you gossiping or deceiving others—what's to stop you from doing the same to them? Finally, have the courage to admit when you've made a mistake or when you truly don't know the answer. People-pleasers can sometimes say what they think others want to hear, but if this is perceived as a lack of integrity, it will backfire and weaken trust.
- **Don't flip flop.** People who are easily influenced are simply not as trustworthy; others can sense that their loyalties might shift in an instant. Where possible, stay true to your convictions and don't allow peer pressure or fashion to weaken or undermine your beliefs. In this instance, it's not boring to be predictable. It signals maturity and integrity.
- **Be there in their time of need.** Some people love being helpful and kind—but only on their terms. True dependability means a person is there for you when it actually counts. Stay alert to what is happening in your social network. How are people? What do they need? The more genuinely available you are, the more people will trust you.

- **Do your work well.** When you take pride in the quality, veracity and integrity of your work, whatever it is, it conveys a powerful sense of self-respect and trustworthiness to others—even if they're not connected to you in a professional capacity. If people have faith in your competence to do a good job, they may find it easier to rely on you in other areas.

Action step: Do you want to be that person that others can count on? It's easy - think in terms of *providing emotional safety*. When they take a tiny emotional risk towards you, be the person who acknowledges, honors and reciprocates that risk—every single time.

Be intellectually humble

There is a deep irony in our culture: we value intelligence and knowledge, yet we don't always value the only proven process for *acquiring* that knowledge and intelligence. To put it another way, we like the finished product of learning, but don't like to be seen grappling with the actual process of learning!

We can all hold unconscious beliefs around what makes a person interesting, valuable, or respectable. What makes them worth *listening* to.

Without realizing it, we can hold an unconscious expectation: *If I want people to like me and listen to me, I have to...*

- Tell everyone what I think and know
- Appear smart or well-educated
- Know the right answer
- Be certain and confident about what I'm saying
- Have the correct opinion
- Be witty, clever or sharp
- Be able to "defend" my position or even convince others of it

The truth? These assumptions and expectations are exactly backward. In reality, ***intellectual humility* is most likely to make you seem likeable, trustworthy, competent and yes, intelligent.**

What is intellectual humility?

Porter & Schumann (2018) authored a paper in the journal Self and Identity, titled "Intellectual Humility and Openness to the Opposing View." According to them, intellectual humility has two parts:

1. Recognition of one's own intellectual limits.
2. Appreciation of other people's intellectual strengths.

It's about **openness**—i.e., being open to the fact that you don't know everything, but also open to the fact that the person you're talking to might know a little something.

Porter and Schumann conducted four separate studies:

- **Study 1 and 2:** Participants took tests to measure their intellectual humility levels (IH) then were asked to think about disagreements about controversial topics. People higher in IH tended to engage more fully and intelligently with all topics.
- **Study 3:** Participants rated their positions concerning certain political topics like abortion or gun control. Various options were offered via Mechanical Turk. The researchers observed that those with higher IH actually spent more time browsing through opposing options, demonstrating that they were actively engaged with them.
- **Study 4:** The researchers primed participants to adopt a *growth mindset*, i.e., the belief that intelligence is not a fixed trait but one acquired through learning and effort. This priming had a measurable effect on people's IH, which in turn influenced the way they engaged with competing viewpoints and ideas.

The overall finding? **Intellectual humility doesn't just make a person more receptive to true learning; it also makes them more likeable.** Why? Because by being open to other viewpoints, you ae demonstrating that you are open to *other people*.

Intellectual humility signals a willingness and capacity to engage, interact, collaborate and understand.

It signals an inclination to consider someone else's worldview, to adapt, to self-correct, and to have enough humility to accept your faults and mistakes.

These are **pro-social attitudes** that are strongly associated with social harmony and cohesion, so it's no wonder that seeing them in other people would make us think, "This person doesn't see things exactly like I do… but you can talk to them. They're reasonable. I like them."

How can you convey to others that you're this type of person? How can you cultivate more intellectual humility?

- Firstly—and this is a BIG one—**do not assume that you already have it!** You can test just how intellectually humble you are by asking yourself these questions:
  o Do I readily admit when I'm wrong or don't know the answer?
  o Do I easily correct / change / adjust my view when I know better?
  o Am I genuinely curious about what other people think?
- **Adopt a growth mindset**. Remind yourself that intelligence is not an inborn part of your identity, but an attitude: the mindset that

sees growth as a process. Value effort, not static traits.
- **Dialogue constructively**. Shift the way you see conversation—and even disagreement:
  - Remember that you have nothing to prove, nor does the other person need your permission, validation or approval.
  - Conversation is not a competition, battle, or pageant. Instead, think of it as a game, a partner dance, a mutual exploration, or a co-creation
  - Difference is not a problem. In fact, it can be a rich source of learning, growth and insight.
  - Say, "I hadn't thought of that before."
- **Be open.**
  - Instead of making statements, ask questions.
  - Instead of defending and justifying your position, deliberately look for your blind spots.
  - Be agnostic—if you don't know, you don't know. Remember you don't always *have to* have an opinion. Withold judgment.
  - Be less concerned with the right answers and opinions, and pay more attention to the process of arriving there.

Think carefully about the people you like, trust and admire the most. Chances are you don't feel this way about them just because they're smart or know all the answers! Rather, you enjoy being with them. It's not that you find them interesting, but that *you* feel more interesting (and interested) when you're with them.

Action step: The next time you feel intellectually insecure, remind yourself of what people truly value in social situations: presence, authenticity, engagement, empathy and a real ability to listen. **This is emotional and relational intelligence.**

The actor-observer bias

In 1973, Michael Storms conducted a thought-provoking series of experiments into what is now known as the **actor-observer bias** ("Videotape and the Attribution Process: Reversing Actors' and Observers' Points of View", *Journal of Personality and Social Psychology*).

To understand why his work is now considered foundational, let's look at exactly how he structured his studies:

- First, 120 undergraduates (all male) were put into two pairs:
    o Two *actors* had an unstructured "getting to know you" conversation.
    o Two *observers* watched.
- All participants were filmed, and were aware they were being filmed.
- After talking, participants (both actors and observers) were asked to complete a questionnaire where they would rate certain behaviors of themselves and others. They rated:

- Friendliness
- Talkativeness
- Nervousness
- Dominance
- They were also asked to attribute these behaviors, i.e., make a guess about what each of the above four behaviors was influenced by:
    - Was it more down to personality traits, disposition and individual character traits?
    - Or was it more down to situational factors—for example, the fact that they were nervous being filmed, or knew it was an experiment?

Storms also changed up a key variable, namely visual perspective—what the participants actually saw, i.e., the perspective of the videotape.

There were three possibilities:

- One group saw no video replay footage.
- A second group saw footage that was the same point of view as they had during the experiment.
- A third group saw footage from a reversed perspective:
    - Actors watched the video focusing on *the other person* in the interaction.

- Observers watched the actor from the actor's own perspective.

Now, while this is a somewhat complicated setup, the findings are noteworthy. Storms found, in general that:

- **Actors** tended to attribute their own behavior **to situational factors**.
- **Observers** tended to attribute actors' behavior **to personal dispositions.**

To clarify, this means that an actor might say, "I felt nervous because it was a strange situation and I didn't know the other guy" (attributing his nervousness to the situation). On the other hand, an observer might view this actor and say about him, "He looks like a nervous kind of guy" (attributing his nervousness to his personality).

Most interestingly, the third group, the one who saw videotape footage from a reversed perspective, showed the opposite of the above finding.

Storms explained it this way: people tend to make attributions (i.e., explain causality) according to what they can see, and what is most immediately in their field of awareness. **The actor-observe bias can be counteracted simply by changing a person's point of view—quite literally!**

Here's how we can apply these findings:

- **Be aware the bias exists.** We automatically judge and understand our own behavior using completely different standards than we do the behavior of others. We might say that we behaved badly because we were having a difficult day, but they behaved badly because they're just a bad person. Simply being aware of the bias, however, will go a long way to minimizing its effects.
- **To be more empathetic, switch lenses.** The terms "point of view" and "perspective" indicate that there really is something special about *seeing* things through another person's eyes. Deliberately switching into other people's perspectives mean you can see them how they see themselves—and how *they* attribute their own behavior.
  - If you think "He's a bad person", for example, then conflict is inevitable.
  - Instead think, "From his perspective, he behaved that way because of his circumstances. From his perspective, my judgment of him is unfair." This will lead to more empathy and understanding.
- **Rewind the tape.** When conflict or misunderstanding rears its head, pause, rewind the tape and watch the situation again, but from their perspective. Have you been unfairly making personality attributions? Is there something in the context that explains their behavior? This

makes you less reactive and far more likely to re-establish harmony and connection.

Action step: When you next catch yourself making personality attributions, see if you can gently consider a situational attribution instead.

If you see a child having a tantrum in the supermarket, for example, instead of assuming that the child is a brat and the mother a poor parent, consider that you're only seeing a very tiny slice of their lives. Put yourself in their shoes and consider how *you'd* explain this situation if you were in it. "This isn't how it normally is. Billy's a good kid. He's just been unwell today, that's all."

How long does it take to make a friend?

We all know that good things take time to evolve… but how much time?

Jeffrey Hall is a communication studies professor at the University of Kansas, and he wanted to identify just how long it takes for relationships to form (Hall, 2019, *Journal of Social and Personal Relationships*).

To investigate, he surveyed 355 adults who had just moved home, asking them how much time they spent with new friends, and how close they felt to those friends.

He also conducted a second study where he monitored 112 university students across a nine-week period. The students reported back after every social encounter, stating how much time they had spent with a new acquaintance, as well as how close they felt to them.

Hall's finding led him to identify four broad categories:

- Acquaintance
- Casual friend
- Friend
- Good friend

He also tried to identify how long it would take to transition from group into the next one. He concluded:

- To go from acquaintance to casual friend → 40 to 60 hours
- To go from casual friend to friend → 80 to 100 hours
- To go from friend to good friend → 200 or more hours

As you can imagine, there are some important caveats and insights here.

As with so much in life, **quality matters, not just quantity.** Time spent doesn't have to be intense and prolonged… but it does have to be **engaged, frequent, reciprocal and intentional.**

You probably don't need to be told what constitutes real bonding time, but here's a list of things that don't quite make the cut:

- Anything obligatory or forced.
- Superficial small talk for the sake of politeness.
- Parallel activities where there is no real interaction or feedback (such as co-watching).

As a rule, boding activities tend to get more intense and more varied the longer they go on, and the closer two people become.

Socially successful people don't rush or force things. They have realistic expectations about how long good connections take to grow, and they're willing to wait. A few things to keep in mind:

- **Be patient; be mindful of the stage you're at**. It's not possible to go directly from acquaintance to good friend. You need to warm up gradually, and to build trust and liking one step at a time. Go slowly and recognize that the other person may be moving at a different pace to you.
- **Match activity to stage.** Are you still acquaintances or casual friends? Save the heavy stuff for later and build rapport by just hanging out, chatting, joking, or doing something fun together. Emotional vulnerability and personal disclosure are valuable, but should be reserved for good friends.
- **Recognize that not everyone will become a friend.** It's OK for some people to remain

acquaintances or casual friends. In fact, it's the norm! Consider the friend pathway a funnel—very few will become good or best friends.
- **Closeness comes in waves.** You may find that friendship takes its own path, and there are times when it races ahead, moves backwards or plateaus.
- **It's a process, not an outcome.** There's no need to rush. Enjoy the process and give things room to unfold. Slow and steady wins; 200 hours spread out over two or three years will produce a more stable friendship than a whirlwind attachment.

In short, *friendship is a time investment.*

Be patient, because there really are no shortcuts. Every little moment of connection is a deposit you make into that bank account.

Action step: If you're feeling frustrated at the pace of development in some friendships, try to count up the total hours you've actually spent together. Putting a number on things can help us maintain more realistic expectations of where we are, and remind us to be patient, and keep on investing that time.

Mollenhorst's Seven-Year Friendships

Gerald Mollenhorst is a Dutch sociologist and friendship researcher who conducted an interesting longitudinal study:

- He surveyed a representative sample of 1000 people ranging in age from 18 to 65 years of age, asking them about their friendships.
- He then followed up with them seven years later (around 600 of them were available to re-interview) and again asked about those same friendships.

Interestingly, Mollenhorst found that on average, **half of people's close friends were no longer in their network after seven years.**

Only around a third of the interviewed participants still claimed the same person as their closest, most trusted friend and confidante.

Is there someone you feel especially close to right now? Well, Mollenhorst's study suggests that there's a strong chance that this person won't be in your life in seven years' time.

Putting it differently: if you take a look at your social network as it stands today, you can expect around half of it to be gone in seven years...

But wait! It's not as depressing as it looks.

Mollenhorst explains that it's the *context* in which we first interact with friends that makes all the difference. Take a look at the kind of questions he asked his interviewees:

- Who do you go to with your most personal issues?

- Where and how did you first meet this person?
- Where and how do you meet up with them now?
- Who helps you out with life's difficulties?
- Who do you casually pop in to visit?

As you might have guessed, Mollenhorst was trying to understand if there was any connection between how you first meet someone, and how likely they are to stick around in your life for the long term.

His findings? Our friendships groups are not built purely on our own personal choice, but also opportunity.

We connect with the people we *can* connect with, i.e., people choose friends and partners from their available possibilities. Friends, he explains, are usually made in shared environments, like at work, around the neighborhood, in school, at church or in social groups.

BUT this may mean that when the context changes... so do the friendships!

- **The "seven-year reshuffle" is normal**, and not a sign that you're doing anything wrong. Even good friendships can have a self-life.

- **Keep making new friends.** Unless you are also replenishing lost friends at the same rate, your social network will steadily dwindle over time.

- **Circumstantial ties often dissolve as life circumstances change**. Good and even great friends may drift from life when contexts change—e.g. people move, change jobs, or get married. Where possible, build a friendship on shared values and connection, and not just shared circumstances.

- **Lifelong friends are rare.** Around a third of friendships survive beyond 7 years, and who knows how many survive repeated seven-year rounds. If you have a very dear friend, *hold on to them!*

- **Stay local.** You're more likely to stay connected to people who are plugged into the same social context and environment as you are. It may be tempting to seek kindred souls from far afield, but you may be less likely to maintain those bonds over time.

- **Make the best of the friendships you have.** Finally, bearing in mind Jeffrey Hall's 200+ hours to make a good friend, don't take too long—try to get those quality, intentional hours in before a life change threatens an existing connection! Deep and meaningful connections are more likely to withstand context change than superficial bonds.

Action step: Are you mourning a dead friendship that didn't stand after circumstances changed? It might be time to give yourself permission to move on. Socially intelligent people are patient and value their friendships. They also know when to close one chapter of life and open the next one.

Conclusion

Let's pull everything together. What have we learned?

- Your early childhood and adolescent experiences shape your social capabilities, but it's never too late to learn to convey warmth, have good boundaries and self-regulate.
- Be honest about limiting beliefs, and adopt more realistic expectations about what social success actually means.
- Understand the biases that may be holding you back. People probably like you more than you think, and are far happier to help you than it may appear.
- Want to be popular? Find out what's valuable to your social group, then align yourself with that, while staying true to yourself when it matters.
- Drop comparison and think positively—it will become a social self-fulfilling prophecy.
- Consciously choose to present yourself in the best light: smile, speak well, transmit good vibes, and consistently put your focus on what you have in common with others.
- It's not about perfection. It's about connection, responsiveness, and flow.
- Friendships take time, and they're built up by frequent low-stakes encounters, shared experiences, and consistent, mutual effort.

- Watch your language. Say people's names, use the word "warm" and be mindful of how your tone and expression influences others.
- Be aware of how you frame things. Humor, pride and humility all have their place—when used in the right way.
- Don't talk too much, or too little. Stay balanced. Conversations need to breathe and flow. Use follow-up questions wherever possible. Advice is good if it's collaborative, but toxic positivity is never welcome.
- Be polite, don't force or fake anything, and be willing to conform—except when it comes to strong moral convictions.
- In the dating market, be original, take pride in yourself, and meet face-to-face when you can. Recognize that relationships are made of many different components—understand which ones and you empower yourself to make proactive changes.
- Social intelligence and mastery can be acquired. Be realistic and pragmatic about *everyone* who comes into your life, not just romantic partners or friends. Be responsive, engaged, open-minded and adaptable. Don't just help people when they're down, but celebrate their wins, too.
- Decide that you are willing to do what's required to be a socially successful person. Cultivate reliability, intellectual humility, the ability to consider other perspectives, patience, dedication and, when necessary,

the ability to move on when a friendship has run its course.

In this book we've taken a brief but focused look at what social science research can tell us about love, relationships and effective social skills. Some findings are fairly obvious… others are an unexpected challenge to the conventional wisdom.

Though a well-designed scientific research study can certainly teach us a lot, when it comes to social skills, **the best laboratory you have is your own life.**

The best way to learn to socialize is to socialize.

Adopt a growth mindset, be genuinely curious about other people, and go out there and try things. Be brave, do experiments, gather data and see for yourself which of these techniques works best in *your* unique social circumstances.

Remember that with a little patience, resilience and self-compassion, you can also be honest about what *doesn't* work, adjust, and try again.

Each of us is a perfectly unique and individual human being. By reading this book you've taken steps to bolster your blind spots and weakness. At the same time, don't forget that you also possess unique social strengths and capabilities. By mastering better social skills, you learn to bring that value more fully into the world. And that's a beautiful thing.

www.ingramcontent.com/pod-product-compliance
Lightning Source LLC
Chambersburg PA
CBHW060556080526
44585CB00013B/579